GOLDSEEKERS

GOLDSEEKERS

Ralph Hall

1978

SONO NIS PRESS

1745 BLANSHARD STREET, VICTORIA, BRITISH COLUMBIA

Copyright © 1978 by Ralph Hall

Canadian Cataloguing in Publication Data

Hall, Ralph.
   Goldseekers

   ISBN 0-919462-72-3 pa.

   1. Hall, Ralph. 2. Gold miners —
British Columbia — Biography. 3. Gold
mines and mining — British Columbia —
History. I. Title.

   FC3826.9.G6H34   971.1′03′0924   c78-002197-5
   F1089.04H34   *

First Printing November 1978
Second Printing September 1979

Published by
SONO NIS PRESS
Victoria, British Columbia

Design: Bev Leech

Printed and bound in Canada by
MORRISS PRINTING COMPANY LTD.
Victoria, British Columbia

I

DEDICATE

THIS BOOK TO THE MEMORY OF

Bill Timms & Ernie Floyd

Contents

Illustrations and Appendices

Introduction

Although this book covers a little publicized period of the mining industry in British Columbia, it is not intended to be an historical record. Rather, it is an attempt — as seen through the eyes of one of many who took part — to convey to the reader, the sights and sounds of a unique period in the placer fields of north central British Columbia. This is a true story. All the characters are real people who, collectively, contributed so much to the Fort St. James-Manson Creek-Germansen area.

Before the present road was completed in 1939 from the Nation River to Manson Creek, every type of transportation was used over the old Baldy Mountain Trail. British Columbia will never again see, in one mining area, the likes of Bob Watson and his dog team, "Skookum" Davidson and his pack horses, Earl Buck and his wagon teams, Bill Faith and his "cat" train, Harold Perison and the Blackburn Brothers with their trucks, and Sheldon Luck, Grant McConachie, Russ Baker with their airplanes. In the depth of winter and during the spring break-up, the Baldy Trail was a severe test for men, animals, and machines. Flying conditions among the mountains, too, were less than ideal on numerous occasions. In many respects it was an amazing period of activity during the Great Depression years.

Despite the influx of hundreds of men from all walks of life, crime was almost non-existent. Cabin doors were left unlocked and the word "vandalism" was unknown.

In this present world of change, it is highly improbable the placer fields of the area — despite the sevenfold increase in the price of gold — will ever again see so much activity. Government regulations, and various environmental groups combined, make it almost impossible.

R.H./1978

9

Acknowledgements

My sincere thanks to Mrs. Sally Faith, Dr. Stuart S. Holland, and Mr. Sheldon Luck for the loan of many of the photographs appearing in this book.

Definitions

ADIT: Commonly but incorrectly called a tunnel.

BARRING DOWN: Removing loose rock left in the roof and walls of a tunnel or adit after blasting operations.

LAGGING: Round or split poles, or planking driven over and along the sides of the supporting timbers to prevent caving in unsafe ground.

CROSSCUT: A narrow exploratory drift, usually at right angles to the main working face of the adit.

SINGLE-JACKING: One person using a drill steel to bore holes in a rock face by striking the end of the steel with a four or six pound hammer.

DOUBLE-JACKING: Two people working together, one holding the drill steel and turning it, while the other strikes the end with a ten to fourteen pound sledge hammer.

CHURN-DRILLING: One person using a long drill steel to bore holes in a downward direction, like in shaft sinking. The weight of the drill penetrates the rock, because it is being raised and dropped with a twisting motion.

SNIPER: One who works by hand in shallow gold-bearing gravels.

SLUICE BOX: A device for trapping gold. The gravels are washed through it by a continuous flow of water.

ROCKER: A device for removing gold from gravels where a continuous supply of water is sometimes not available. Used occasionally to test ground before sluice boxes are set up. The rocking motion gradually settles the heavier particles into the riffles and gold, being one of the heaviest, is trapped in the riffles.

RIFFLES: Devices of many designs for trapping gold in the bottom of the sluice box.

MONITOR: A machine, run by water pressure, used in hydraulic mining. A continuous jet of water can be directed in almost any direction by the use of a single lever.

MUCK: Blasted rock, usually containing some mineral. The term is sometimes used to describe paydirt.

PIPER: A monitor operator.

PAYDIRT: River gravel or any gravels containing placer gold.

PLACER GOLD: Gold which at one time was in rock, but through climatic changes, erosion, ice and water action has — over countless centuries of time — been concentrated in old or existing waterways and channels.

COLOURS: Specks of gold.

GROUND-SLUICING: Water, not under pressure, which helps to move paydirt through the sluice boxes.

PENSTOCK: A device for regulating and filtering the water supply from a ditch-line before it enters a hydraulic pipeline.

A Dream of Gold

The year was 1935. Six long years since the start of the period known as the "Great Depression." To many they were dark, desperate days, seemingly without end. Canada, this great land, had stagnated under leaders of little vision and no faith. Thousands of unemployed filled the cities, while other thousands "rode the rods" from one end of the country to the other in the hope that somehow, somewhere, they would be lucky enough to find employment.

Some of the police were harsh and ruthless and, in a few instances, sadistic brutes. Many were the beatings and worse, administered to some transients for no other reason than that they were jobless, broke, and hungry. The order of the day was, "Get out" or "Move on." If you protested you were a "Red." Rioting had shaken several of the larger cities, and only the breadlines and soup kitchens had helped to keep conditions under a semblance of control.

In the country the "Bennett buggy" had replaced the car as a means of transportation. Only government officials and some of the storekeepers could afford to run cars. True, the country people as a whole were better off than the city dwellers, if only due to the fact that they could grow vegetables and quite often kill wild game.

Money, however, was practically nonexistent. The only source was one or two days "relief work" each month for the princely sum of thirty-five cents an hour. This work consisted of manual labour, usually with picks and shovels or axes. Sometimes a few dollars could be earned during the winter months by hacking ties, if you were lucky enough to obtain a small subcontract and a stand of jack pine timber of suitable size.

It was these conditions which faced Bill and I during the spring of 1935. Bill Timms, three years my junior, was in his early twenties. We had been friends and partners for several years. We had worked in relief camps for seven dollars and fifty cents per month and had tried our hand at cowpunching in the Cariboo country. Never had we quit a job. We had always been laid off when the work was completed.

We found nothing glamorous about the cowboy's life. It was nothing but hard, long, dirty work with very little pay at the end of each month. The cattle business, like almost everything else at that time, was extremely depressed. The very choicest beef was selling on the hoof at two and one-half cents per pound, if buyers could be found to take it at that price. No, we decided, the cowboy's life was not for us. It only lasted from haying time to fall round-up, or about four months' work each year. No cattlemen could afford to keep all their hands the year round.

At that time our homes were at Chilco, a little place some thirteen miles northeast of Vanderhoof, approximately the centre of British Columbia. It was mostly jack pine land, with some wild hay meadows. It was hard to raise any kind of grain or vegetable crop, because the soil, for the most part, was very silty. After plowing and discing, the first good rainfall would cause it to set in a cement-like state, which would prevent further rainfall from penetrating to any depth. Almost inevitably the potato crop was killed by summer frosts. The only vegetable that really thrived was the turnip, so invariably our diet consisted of moose meat and turnips. Rabbits and grouse were plentiful, and once in a while we managed to kill a deer.

Without the wild game our living would have been meagre indeed. Hunting licenses and closed season meant nothing to us, because no game was ever wasted. The meat was shared among many families. If it was summertime when killed, it was immediately canned, because there were no deep freezers in those days. If it was wintertime we hung it outside or in the woodshed where it was soon frozen solid. We were getting by or "existing" would be a better word, but a deadend road is not the road the young fellow usually cares to travel.

Bill and I spent many evenings discussing what, if anything, we could do to bring about an improvement in the seemingly hopeless situation of our present lives. We were single and each of us was drawing down the princely sum of two dollars and eighty cents, because we were allowed one day's relief work each month.

We had tried to find permanent jobs to the east and west of our homes with no luck at all. We did a little better to the south in the Cariboo cattle country, but the job barely lasted four months. Our travelling expenses on the return home had used what little money we had managed to save, so we arrived at Chilco with the same amount we had when we had left some months before.

For years we had heard stories of the Omineca gold fields to the north, but to us it was a fabled land and might as well have been on another planet. After all, we had been assured by the old-timers that it would take at least two hundred dollars for a pack horse and an outfit, because there was nothing but wild, barren country beyond Fort St. James. Two hundred dollars! What a laugh! Might as well be two million as far as we were concerned. We could never save two hundred dollars for equipment and food to make a trip to that country. Besides, we were greenhorns where gold was concerned — did not even know what the stuff looked like in its raw state. Still, the idea of someday making a trip to that far-off part of British Columbia fascinated us, as gold and the stories of gold have fascinated men for centuries.

Then in April of 1935, we heard rumours. Rumours that the Consolidated Mining and Smelting Company was going to start a mine in Manson Creek. Could this be true? We determined to find out and hiked the thirteen miles to Vanderhoof to get some information. Maybe we would be chasing another will-o'-the-wisp, but we had done that before and did not expect too much. We had to find out, because we reasoned a mine needs men to operate it. We were young and tough and maybe we could find employment. Maybe! Life had been full of "maybes" for years.

It was true! No doubt about it. The man who ran the freight truck between Vanderhoof and Fort St. James told us all he knew about it. Yes, the mine would employ fifty men when it started operation. Perhaps more. What news this was. What great news!

Bill and I returned to Chilco, discussing the good luck which we felt had been ours, and never noticed the thirteen miles which passed underfoot. In our optimistic mood we were already digging gold by the shovelful for this C. M. & S. Company, whoever they might be. Boy! What could we do with all that money? Seventy-five dollars a month and free board! Sure, we had to work seven days a week for it, but who cared about that? It was a job, and a good one too. We really would be "stakey" when we came back to Chilco after a few months in the north. Castles in the air — we built a million of them. Not for a minute did we consider that things might not work out as we hoped they would.

The Decision

After telling the folks at home of our decision to go north, we started planning in earnest for our trek to Utopia, some one hundred and seventy miles away. First, we had to have pack-boards. They were the only thing for carrying loads. The weight was on the shoulders, where it was best supported, and not on the back. Why had they not been made before? It seemed they had come into general use only since the Depression.

Buying a couple of pack-boards was out of the question. What little money we had saved from the previous winter's work of hacking two hundred and fifty ties had to be carefully conserved. We had pooled our money, agreed on partnership, and found we could raise twenty-eight dollars and fifteen cents between us. We figured if we made our own pack-boards, we could make the trip on about three dollars each for grub, which would consist mostly of hardtack, rice, raisins, and a can of sweetened milk for our tea. We would have liked to have included a .22 rifle for killing small game, but had to consider the extra weight and abandoned the idea. We would take along a couple of extra bucks just in case we did not find a job and ran short of grub for the return trip. We would buy it from the mining company — or so we thought!

Had we known what was in store for us, we might never have started. But being complete greenhorns and blissfully ignorant about anything to the north, we quickly made our final preparations before departure.

The First Trip

The day was perfect. Blue sky overhead with not a trace of cloud anywhere. It was still cool and the sun was barely above the eastern horizon when we started on the first leg of our long hike. Our packs were not heavy, because we had not purchased our grub. They consisted only of our bedrolls and personal toiletries — soap, towel, razor, toothbrush. Sleeping bags or eiderdowns were beyond our limited means. My bedroll consisted of two grey blankets with natural sheep's wool sewn between them. These were wrapped in a canvas, approximately seven feet square, which could be used either as a ground sheet or fly depending on the weather conditions. Bill's bedroll was similar except that his blankets were separate and had no sheep's wool. The pack-boards were riding nicely on our shoulders. With light hearts and the sun at our backs on a beautiful morning of mid-May 1935, we left Chilco and set our faces toward Vanderhoof, our first stop.

We arrived there in good time. In fact, the few stores were barely opened for business. First we went for breakfast to the O.K. Hotel cafe which was run by everyone's friend Wong Chuey. How many men "Chuey" had helped in those days will never be known. He was a big man by Chinese standards, being about six feet and probably two hundred and twenty pounds. He never turned away anyone who was in dire need of a meal. He had helped us a few years before on a futile trip west, when we had only ten cents between us. Not only did he give us a meal, but when we left he handed us a loaf of bread.

After our meal, for which we were in a position to pay this time, and the usual chat with Chuey, we went around to Breen's store to buy food for the trip north. After purchase, this was divided and half was placed on each pack. Then we weighed each pack, complete with board. Bill's weighed in at sixty-one pounds and mine at sixty-three, the difference being the sheep's wool between my blankets. In addition, we each carried a small hand axe.

17

After helping each other to place the packs squarely on our shoulders, we set our faces to the north and Fort St. James, some forty-one miles away. We had agreed before we left that we would take it fairly easy, at the beginning that is. We would walk for an hour and rest for ten minutes or so. As we toughened up and the packs got lighter, due to the consumption of the food, we would lengthen the time between the rest periods. We figured to take a day and a half to reach Fort St. James, because our packs would be heavier at first.

The day was now turning quite warm, with the sun beating down from a cloudless sky. We were glad to take a rest after the first hour, and the perspiration was beginning to flow freely from our bodies. We did not remove the packs, but rested the bottom of them on fallen trees to remove the weight sufficiently from our shoulders and backs. The packs acted as props or supports for the upper part of the body. It was a very comfortable position for resting, when the legs were straight out, and we learned to doze in that position on the numerous occasions we used it. We had found the road dry in the centre once we had crossed the bridge over the Nechako River on the north side of Vanderhoof, but very badly rutted and not a good walking surface for backpacking.

After a ten minute rest we started walking again. By the time another hour had passed we were soaked in perspiration and very thirsty. Like the greenhorns we were, we had completely forgotten about drinking and had packed our tin cups along with our other utensils. Of course we could have opened one of the packs, but that would have delayed us some, and there was plenty of running water beside the road.

Finally we came to a bridge which crossed a good-sized creek, and there we found several empty tobacco tins. Others had evidently camped here recently, leaving much evidence that it was a favourite stopping place for eating. We washed one of the cans and drank our fill of the cold water from the creek. From then on we kept that tobacco can handy at all times, and it accompanied us all the way to our journey's end.

On our third lap, we began to encounter hilly conditions and did not make such good time. Also, the lacing on the pack-board canvas had stretched sufficiently to allow the wooden framework to rub our bodies. We had to stop and tighten the lacing, otherwise our backs would soon have been raw and sore.

18

We had completed this and were busy helping each other replace the packs when suddenly a new sound burst upon us. It was a truck motor labouring up one of the hills behind us. We stood and watched the road and, sure enough, a truck appeared over the brow of the hill about a half-mile back. The best thing we could do was keep walking and hope the driver would stop and offer us a lift. That is exactly what he did, after enquiring how far we were going.

Another man and a woman shared the cab with him, but there was room for us at the back, even though he was heavily loaded. We certainly appreciated the lift, because the going was very rough, even for the truck. As we got nearer Fort St. James, numerous soft spots in the roadway began to appear, and in many places the spring run-off water was running across it. Several times the wheels appeared bogged down, but each time the truck managed to pull out under its own power.

Finally, about sixteen miles from the Fort, the wheels went down and stayed down. No amount of jockeying could budge them an inch. The driver had been prepared for this and produced three husky jacks, short pieces of plank, two shovels, two axes, and a mattock. He also had a coil of strong rope and a couple of big hooks. Fortunately we did not require all this equipment. By jacking up the wheels and digging out enough dirt to put some of the short planking and brush under the wheels, we managed to get the truck to firmer road.

Bill and I worked hard because we figured we owed it to the driver for giving us a lift. We were dirty and muddy, but did not mind because we knew our journey would be no picnic. Climbing on the back of the truck we continued the rough, bumpy trip. Several times the driver stopped and looked over soft places on the road before making an attempt to drive over them. Each time, we got off the truck deck and walked over the bad places with the two people from the cab. Good fortune was with us, because the truck did not completely bog down again. With sighs of relief we saw the settlement of Fort St. James ahead.

Around four-thirty p.m. we stopped in front of the Hudson's Bay store. Only then did we realize how hungry we were. We had not eaten anything since leaving Chuey's in Vanderhoof that morning.

Replacing the packs on our shoulders again, we thanked the driver for the lift and he thanked us for the help we had given when the truck was mired. We were quite happy to reach Fort St. James almost a day ahead of our schedule. Our immediate concern was finding a camping place, building a fire, and cooking some food. We did not have far to look.

A creek, lined by huge spruce trees, flowed at the foot of a hill in almost the centre of the settlement. We could see quite a number of men camped there. Some had canvas sheets for shelter, others had made brush lean-tos. Several campfires were burning. It was almost suppertime. At least two parties were preparing some kind of a meal. Bill and I walked over. As we passed, everyone greeted us pleasantly and some even cheerfully.

Truly, the Great Depression with its hardships had created a feeling of camaraderie and brotherliness among individuals and families that was to completely disappear years later as more money, work, and jobs became available.

Selecting a spruce tree and camp which was now vacant, we took off our packs, lit a fire, and started supper. We were famished — even the hardtack tasted good. When we arrived, we had planned to stay overnight in the Fort. But now, after a meal and a rest, we wondered if we should push on. There was still lots of daylight left for travelling.

Some of the transients who had greeted us visited with us at our camp, and naturally the conversation got around to what we had planned. Most of the fellows thought we were starting out too early. According to reports, there was still lots of snow on the Baldy Mountain which we had to cross before descending to Manson Creek. Never having travelled north of Fort St. James, this information did not mean much. In our abysmal ignorance about everything ahead of us, we simply could not visualize any conditions which could not be overcome.

In fact, we decided to push on that same evening. Bill said he knew someone named Joe Huffman who had a Model "A" car. Perhaps he could get him to drive us up the north road as far as he could. We could afford this because we had not spent quite as much on food as we previously estimated. Joe was quite agreeable, but said he could only make about four miles north. The road was too soft beyond that point. Well, that would save backpacking four miles, so we climbed into his car.

We were off at last! From now on, once we had left Joe, we would be entering country without any settlements. If we became lost, we would have to rely on our own initiative to get out of any unpleasant situations in which we found ourselves. True, thousands had trekked this part of the country during the great gold rush of 1870-71, but their very numbers had been the means of saving many on the trail. Even so, some had left their homes never to return.

The road was rutted and bumpy for the short ride with Joe. He left us after four miles, for which we paid him fifty cents, and returned to the Fort. We made camp under the jackpines and crawled under the blankets. What a relief to relax after that first strenuous day! Sleep did not come easily, despite being bone-tired. Maybe we were still excited by the thoughts of the trip ahead, or perhaps we had overdone things the first day. After a long period of restless turning, we finally passed into sound sleep. We were up early! It was a new day and we were anxious to get going.

After a hurried breakfast we broke camp, threw on our packs, and strode out like giants refreshed. We were to learn a bitter lesson in just a few hours, which taught us to take things easier in future.

The road surface was rough for walking and we encountered numerous soft spots in the first six miles. The weather was still good and it was great to be outdoors that early May morning. About ten miles north of the Fort, we came to a large-sized creek which was spanned by a low log bridge. The brown water was rushing at a tremendous rate just a few inches beneath, and we could feel the bridge vibrating under our feet as we crossed. Once on the other side, we threw off our packs, had a drink and our fifteen minute rest. It was another cloudless day and already we were beginning to feel the heat.

I could not help thinking as we rested, how much more fortunate we were than our city brothers. They had nothing to look forward to but handouts or the soup kitchens. Having been raised near or living in big cities most of my life, I found the vastness of this Omineca country fascinating. There was still a sense of adventure here and the chance of a pot of gold at the rainbow's end. I knew I could never live in a big city again. My daydreams were suddenly shattered by Bill's announcement that it was time to get moving again. About a mile beyond the creek, the road suddenly straightened out and, as far as we could judge, seemed endless.

Someone had nailed a piece of board on a jack pine beside the road with the words "Juniper Straight" scrawled on it. That seven miles of straight road, if it could be called a road, had to be seen to be believed. It was seven solid miles of gumbo mud, swampland, and water. What a nightmare! At each step we would sink over the ankles, and as each foot was lifted the mud would stick like glue. We tried walking in the trees and brush alongside, only to run into swamp, water, windfall, and spongy ground. Our packs hampered us, too, because the brush and undergrowth was extremely thick in many places. We just had to take the mud on the open road — there was no alternative. After a couple of hours, in which we travelled less than two miles, other complications developed.

Heel blisters! The effort required to overcome the suction of the mud was actually causing our heels to rub on the backs of our boots. In other words, our feet were lifting inside our boots. This was a problem we had not even thought about when we left home. We had never encountered it anywhere on many long hikes in the past. For hours we plodded on, with the perspiration pouring from our bodies, because by this time the sun was quite hot. We rested when a suitable windfall presented itself by the roadside. I knew the blisters had burst on my heels and there was nothing I could do about it until we made camp.

The road seemed endless! A straight line of road may have been the shortest distance between two points, but it sure was monotonous. We got a change from the mud after six miles. It was water up to the knees and no way around it! It spread in the bush as far as we could see. The willows were so thick on each side at this point that even a moose would have had tough going. Not being moose, we took the water on the open road. There must have been almost half a mile of sloshing through it. At first the cold water had felt good on our burning feet, but by the time we finally crossed, our feet and ankles were feeling numb. What a pleasant surprise greeted us at the other side! Instead of the gumbo surface we were actually walking on sand. How good it felt!

No more heaving and tugging to free our feet. In fact, they felt so light, they did not seem to be part of us. We were exhausted and hungry and decided to have a meal at the next suitable camping ground. It was about a mile and a half ahead where another log bridge spanned a large creek. There were big spruce trees on high, dry ground alongside. A perfect camping place. On a board, nailed to the bridge, was a single word "Tsilcoh."

Our first concern was the condition of our feet. They were not painful and all the blisters had burst. With a little care they should be healed in a couple of days. It was well past noon, so we made tea and had a good meal. It was good to relax beneath those trees, and the day was perfect. We slept and without intending to do so, we passed into complete oblivion for almost four hours. We decided we might just as well spend the remainder of the day there, because it would be hard to find a better place to camp. Besides, our legs and feet needed a good rest and we could already feel the effects of that terrible trek through the gumbo. After a slow and lazy supper, we walked the few yards upstream and leaned on the guardrail of the bridge, watching the swift flow of the creek waters beneath. We wondered idly if there could be fish in it. Again we looked at the sign "Tsilcoh." What did it mean? We knew it must be of the local Carrier language, because there was a large reservation back in Fort St. James.

For a couple of hours we discussed many things, and around sundown we returned to camp. We had already prepared good thick mattresses of spruce boughs which, when properly laid, make one of the best beds in the world. The clean, tangy aroma from the spruce needles is an aid to sleep, if an aid be needed in this vast country. We did not need any, despite our long afternoon nap, and again we fell into a deep sleep almost as soon as we turned in.

It was broad daylight when I woke! Bill carried a pocket watch, so I woke him up to ask what time it was. Five-fifteen a.m. and time to get moving on a new day. However, there was going to be none of the mad rush of the previous one. We had learned our lesson. After a leisurely breakfast of porridge and flapjacks, we loaded up our packs and were on our way. Our leg and thigh muscles were stiff from our exertions in the gumbo mud, but after walking for a short time, they quickly loosened up. The conditions underfoot were much improved, even though we had to skirt the occasional soft spot. More gravel was in evidence and made for a better road surface.

We walked for an hour and rested for ten minutes as we originally planned. The weather had changed somewhat. The sky was full of thunderheads, and looked as if there might be a heavy rain before nightfall. At mile twenty-eight, which had been marked on a board by someone, we had to wade again, but only for about twenty feet. The water covered the road about knee deep.

Around noon we ate a meal consisting mostly of hardtack and raisins, washed down by tea. By suppertime we estimated we had walked twenty-three miles and decided to make camp for the night. We were not too tired, but figured that was enough for the day. The clouds were still very threatening, but no rain had fallen on us. The first thing was to put up the canvas fly and then, of course, make our beds under it. That finished, we prepared supper and relaxed after gathering a little dry wood to start the fire next morning. As usual before turning in, we fell to discussing what we would do with our lives if we found employment at the mine in Manson Creek. We tried to visualize what the mine would look like and how gold was recovered. Well, we would soon know. We planned to be there in three more days and with this in mind we went to our beds.

How much later it was when I awoke I do not know, but the night was still black. The sound of rain on the fly had awakened me. How good it felt to be in a warm dry bed and sheltered by a stout canvas. I turned over and promptly fell asleep. We were up again at five-thirty next morning. The rain had ceased for the time being, although the sky was still overcast. We were hoping to reach the Nation River by suppertime and estimated we had twenty-five miles to go. We had heard much about this river. We knew it drained into the Arctic watershed. From the information we had, gold could be found on some bars and seams of coal outcropped at various places.

We were anxious to see the Nation because that meant we would be more than halfway on our journey from Fort St. James. At first the mud was quite deep, but at least it was not gumbo anymore. The country was changing. It looked more like parkland. Gradually the conditions got better. There was no underbrush at all among the trees, and it was possible to walk among them without difficulty. The ground was carpeted with some kind of a short, springy moss. Altogether, it was very pleasant walking because the roadbed was now composed of natural fine gravel.

One thing that puzzled us was the lack of game birds and animals. We had seen nothing but a few squirrels and whiskey-jacks since leaving the Fort. For some reason, we had anticipated seeing lots of game in the north country. After walking about two hours we came to a campsite. On a tree was nailed a board with "Horseshoe Lake" printed on it. We sat and rested for a while. What a nice, clean place nature had built here. We would have liked to linger, but there was a long trail ahead. With some reluctance, we shouldered our packs and started off again.

We had only travelled half a mile when we saw someone ahead, coming in our direction. Only then did it strike us that here was our first human contact since leaving Fort St. James several days ago. He was a native Indian, who met us with a wide grin and a word of greeting. He was carrying a 30-30 rifle. Neither Bill nor I knew any natives, because there were none where we lived at Chilco. We had a hard time understanding all he said, but we explained that we were going to Manson Creek. He told us he was going to his cabin at Horseshoe Lake, where we had rested, which meant he had not far to travel. Before leaving, we asked him how far it was to the Nation River, and he replied, "Eight miles." At least we thought he said eight miles. We discussed this as we were walking. If this were so, then we were making better time than we had thought.

Gradually the good walking conditions deteriorated until we were in mud and water again. Before us stretched an immense burn. Most of the dead trees had fallen and a young growth of pine had started among the windfalls. Every few yards the trail disappeared under water. Sometimes it was up to the ankles, but more often it was knee-deep. This was tough going! There must be something wrong with our calculations. If the Nation River was only eight miles away, when we left the native, then it should be in sight by now. Instead there stretched this seemingly endless burn, and only faintly could we see where the green timber belt commenced.

On our right was a huge mountain of rock, which must be on the south side of the Nation. Although we walked for several hours, we seemed unable to pass it. Finally, we decided to rest and cook a meal. We took a full hour before putting on our packs and felt much better for the break. Hour after hour we slogged along, that mountain to the right always seemed to be in the same place. First Bill would lead, picking the best place to walk, and I would follow with my head bent, trying to step in the same places he had. After an hour, I would go ahead and he would follow. We made slow progress, but by suppertime we had crossed the burn, which we estimated was at least twelve miles long. We were in the green timber again, and that pesky mountain to the right was out of sight.

We started downgrade at last. Surely the river must be at the bottom — but, no, we started uphill again. Where the heck was the Nation? We must have travelled at least twice the eight miles which we thought the native had told us that morning. Finally we were going down a steep grade. This must be it! It was! We could see the river glistening through the trees as we kept descending. At last we stood on the hand-hewn timbers of the bridge which spanned the river at the narrowest point. A pack train and a crew of men, supervised by O. J. Reid, had erected this bridge in 1931 during the months of October and November.

We had planned on camping overnight at the river, but we felt so elated once we arrived that we decided, after a rest, to push on. About four miles north of the Nation we set up camp for the night. After supper we built a big fire, because it was quite cold after sundown. We were not only travelling north, we were also at a considerably higher altitude.

Before turning in we discussed the day's travel, with an estimate of twenty-nine miles covered. Only then did it dawn on us that it was eighteen miles to the Nation River and not eight as we had thought. We could afford to laugh now about our idiotic mistake. The night was clear and very cold. There was an ample supply of dry wood and we took turns at keeping the fire stoked. We started breakfast next morning at five o'clock. We found ice on our tea pail which had been filled with water the night before.

Soon after six o'clock we were ready to hit the trail. Again the sky was cloudless. All the water holes on the trail were covered with ice, and the sunlight was reflected from millions of frost particles on the trees. It was hard to realize that the month of May was more than half spent.

We were climbing steadily. Soon a mountain creek barred our path. The run-off water was travelling at a tremendous rate, and we could not even think of trying to ford it. Snow from the previous winter still lingered along its banks in several low places. We could chop down a tree to get across it, if we had no other alternative. We decided to scout upstream first and, sure enough, found a natural windfall which crossed over the other side. It was extremely slippery, with a coating of clear ice covering the bark. There were no more than ten feet to walk, but I felt as if I were crossing Niagara Falls on a tight rope. It was a great relief to get on solid footing after that.

Around noon we were suddenly surprised. The trail led to an open area where two small cabins had been built on the bank of a fair-sized creek. Smoke was issuing from the stovepipe of one cabin. We decided to stop because in any case it was a good place to have lunch. Approaching the cabins from the rear we gave a shout to herald our approach. We were sure no one had noticed us. At the shout, a man appeared around the corner of the building and invited us to enter.

There were two men in the cabin. One was very tall and thin. The other, who had welcomed us, was probably the finest looking man I had seen for years. He was about an even six feet tall with the build of an athlete. He had short-cropped blonde hair with a small moustache to match, perfect teeth, and clear blue eyes set in a face which glowed with health. That he was a Scotsman there was no doubt, because his accent could be no other. But his name was pure Anglo-Saxon — Fred Smith. His partner also was definitely a Scot, named Alex Kynoch.

We were rather surprised at their appearance, and I must confess a little ashamed of our own. They were both clean and freshly shaven with newly laundered clothes, while we were just about the opposite. Bill did not grow much of a beard at any time, but mine was very bushy because I had not shaved since leaving the Fort. Our clothing, too, was less than immaculate after all the mud and water we had sloshed through. When we remarked about the differences between us, they assured us that when they arrived at this cabin almost a week ago, they were in worse condition than we were. They were recuperating after a hike from Manson Creek — much of it on snowshoes — and were on their way back to Fort St. James.

They said there was still a lot of snow on the Baldy Mountains. When they crossed, it had been very heavy and wet with rain falling most of the time. Alex, especially, had felt the strain and had had to rest often. When they finally reached the cabins, they decided to recuperate for several days. They assured us that we could not possibly cross Baldy without snowshoes, unless it happened to freeze hard. This news was a blow to us! That what they told us was authentic, there was not the slightest doubt. Yet, it was unthinkable that we could turn back now after travelling so far and enduring so much. We had to keep going — it was as simple as that.

After a meal and rest, we shouldered our packs again. Fred and Alex thought we were being a little foolish, but they shook our hands and wished us the best of luck. They told us about a trapper's cabin some fourteen miles away. If we reached it before nightfall, it would be a good place to sleep. The trail ahead was the usual, except that we now encountered several patches of snow which had not yet melted from the previous winter. It was not deep, however, and we had no difficulty making the fourteen miles to the cabin.

There was a small camp stove in it and two narrow bunks which had some kind of animal hides in place of mattresses. These hides intrigued us. Bill was of the opinion they were caribou. We were only familiar with moose and deer hides. Caribou! Up to now we had vaguely thought they belonged in the land of the Eskimo, yet here was evidence that we were entering caribou country. We were truly travelling north.

After a meal we unrolled our blankets on the bunks and turned in. The first thing we noticed after a few minutes was the gentle warmth of the hides beneath us. It was as though we were lying on blankets which had been warmed in front of a stove. It was amazing, yet we did not wonder about it very long. We both passed into the deep sleep which healthy tiredness induces.

It was broad daylight when I awoke. Bill was still sleeping contentedly, when I glanced at his watch hanging from a wooden peg driven into the log wall. It was not yet five o'clock, so I turned over and promptly went back to sleep. Those bunks were sheer luxury after the previous night, but we could not afford to linger too long.

At six o'clock we started breakfast. While preparing our packs, we fell to discussing the caribou hides again. Why should they be warmer to sleep on than any other hide? We could not come up with a reasonable answer. Before leaving the cabin we arranged it the way we found it, making sure the woodbox was full and there was plenty of dry kindling for anyone who might follow us.

The sky was heavy and dull, and rain was not too far away. We hoped to make the foot of the Baldy Mountain before nightfall. We were gradually climbing to a higher altitude, and it was noticeable in several ways. Not only was there a chill in the air and more frequent patches of snow, but among the trees where there was no snow, a grey, thick moss was very much in evidence.

Animal tracks were now very common, and we knew now for sure that they had been made by caribou. It did not surprise us in the least when we saw four of them on the slope of a hill about a quarter of a mile distant. They were smaller than I had thought when I had judged them from the size of their tracks. Animals seem to know instinctively whether they are being hunted or not and they did not seem too much disturbed by our presence. We watched them for a couple of minutes, then continued on our way.

By now a chill wind was blowing and a light rain falling. It was not bad among the trees, but out in the open it was anything but comfortable. At least we were warm while walking and the packs kept our backs dry.

Towards noon the trail entered more open country. Natural meadows and clearings appeared as the trees became more sparse. Suddenly our attention was turned to a small knoll on the right, just a few yards from the trail. There on top was the grave of some miner of the 1870 era. We walked over and examined the headboard. Still legibly carved was the name "Hugh Gillis." The headboard was propped up. The foot of it had long since decayed, as had the fence which had originally been around the grave.

We stood there in silence, but questions began to enter my mind. We knew his name but nothing apart from that. Who was this man? Where did he come from? Why had he died here? What caused his death? Later, on our arrival in Manson Creek, we were to learn some of the answers.

Evidently, Hugh Gillis and two other men had been mining partners in Manson. Legend has it that they had done reasonably well and were on their way "outside" with around twenty thousand dollars in gold between them. Hugh Gillis intended to marry the girl of his life, who he had vowed to marry when he left her to "strike it rich."

At this point on the trail, when the three partners were having a meal, they were met by a native carrying mail from Fort St. James to Manson Creek. There was a letter for Hugh Gillis from his girl-friend, which he opened and read in silence. Then, not saying a word to the others, he got up, walked a few yards down the trail, put his revolver to his head, and pulled the trigger. His partners buried him on the knoll and erected a small cairn of stones where he had fallen after shooting himself. The letter told the story. The girl he hoped to marry on his return had already married someone else during his absence. To this day his mortal remains lie undisturbed by civilization. A large creek has been named after him to keep alive forever the legend of Hugh Gillis.

Bill and I silently resumed our journey to the foot of Baldy Mountain. It was raining steadily and the conditions underfoot were none too good. Later that afternoon we started to climb a fairly steep grade. At first we thought we were in the mountains because the snow was about eight inches deep, but then we started downgrade again and knew it was only a ridge or hogback we had crossed. We were gradually descending. The trail skirts large boulders of granite deposited by the last ice age.

Suddenly we smelled the smoke of a campfire. It seemed incredible, but we had to believe it. Sure enough, just beyond the lowest point on the trail ahead was a campfire, and under the largest spruce tree a tarp had been stretched. Before the fire was the figure of a man in a semi-crouching position, obviously cooking a meal. We approached him with mixed feelings, because we knew he had seen us even before we had seen him. However, he gave no sign as we approached. Only when we were about thirty feet away did he look up from his cooking and, in a loud, booming voice, greeted us. "Howdy, boys! Welcome to Baldy."

Such was our meeting with "Skookum Davidson," one of the most fantastic characters the north has ever produced. We did not know it then, but here was Sergeant Skook Davidson of World War I and winner of the Military Medal in that conflict. Here was a cowboy, mule-skinner, and packer extraordinary. Here was the person whose life story should be written or dramatized by a Hollywood movie. Skookum stood up in front of the fire. He was big, even without the ten-gallon hat he was wearing. Six feet, four inches tall, with huge shoulders, and a barrel chest. It was easy to see how he had come by his nickname.

Bill and I threw off our packs at Skook's invitation to "sit and shoot the breeze for awhile." Bill and he did most of the talking. What fascinated me most — after Skookum himself — was the huge cast-iron pressure cooker over the fire. Somehow it seemed out of character with this big man who appeared capable of eating his meat raw.

Finally my curiosity got the better of me and I asked why he used it. Skookum turned to me and, knowing what a greenhorn I was, gave me a half-pitying look. "Son, at this altitude, I could boil these danged beans forever in a can, and they would still be like rocks. I like 'em cooked, son." I did not ask any more foolish questions.

After awhile Bill and I decided to have supper. By now our food supply was almost exhausted and we only had some hardtack and raisins left. However, there were only twelve miles "over the hump" to travel before reaching Manson Creek, so we were not worried. We could buy food at the mine if we did not find work — so we thought. Skook noticed our skimpy food, so he told us to help ourselves to the beans. They were really good and soft, too, thanks to the pressure cooker.

He also told us there were three to six feet of snow over Baldy, and that unless it froze hard we could not possibly make it. He was waiting for a dog team and sleigh to come over from the mine to pick up supplies he had brought in by pack train.

The rain had ceased by now, so Bill and I had to think about a camp for the night. Across a snow-filled draw, a hundred yards away, was a trapper's cabin. It looked as if it had been abandoned for years, but we decided to go over. The snow was much deeper than we thought. We quickly sank to the waist. We could not walk, or force our way through, because the snow was too heavy and wet from the rain. There was only one way to travel and that was on our stomachs, laying our bodies full length on the snow.

What a struggle! It took us a long time to wiggle and claw our way to the cabin, but eventually we made it. It was not too bad inside, and although there were holes in one end of the roof, the other was okay. Soon we had a fire going and it made things much more cheerful. We spread out our bedrolls and relaxed. Somehow it never occurred to us that we might have to stay here a long time unless it froze hard enough for us to walk on the snow over Baldy. About nine o'clock, although still daylight, we decided to turn in. The sky looked clear in the west, but there was still no sign of frost.

It seemed I had hardly closed my eyes when I felt Bill shaking me. "Wake up! Wake up! There's something coming." There was a shuffling noise close by the cabin. Then we heard someone grunt. It was a human sound, so we did not get up. The moon was shining as two men opened the door and came in. We struck a match and they saw us. Throwing more wood on the open fire, they started to spread their bedrolls by its light. The shuffling noise Bill had heard was these two fellows travelling on their stomachs, much the same as we had done. There was a crust on the snow. It had started to freeze, but it was not strong enough to support them by walking.

We introduced ourselves and they told us they were heading for Manson. They had heard about a mine opening up and thought there might be employment.

Evidently we all had the same idea. Bill and I had journeyed from Chilco, but these boys had come in from the prairies. They were Hungarians and both had the same Christian name. The blonde fellow was Mike Meyer and the dark fellow was Mike

31

Zalitach. They were soon to be known to everyone in the north as "Boiler" Mike and "Grizzly" Mike. How they came by these names will be explained later. After talking awhile, comparing notes about our hike from Fort St. James, we settled down to get some sleep.

It must have been around three a.m. when I got up to test the snow. It was freezing hard. It felt almost like pavement. Even when I jumped on it, I could not punch through. Boy, what good luck this was! The sky was clear of all cloud and there was a little moon-light. I went in the cabin and aroused Bill, because we could not afford to lose any time. We must be over the hump of Baldy before the sun got hot enough to soften the snow.

Throwing the packs on our backs we started out, after telling the two Mikes about the snow conditions over the summit. They decided to rest a little longer. They were very tired, having got to the foot of the mountain much later than we.

It was good walking! Where we had wriggled on our stomachs a few hours previously, we could now step out with confidence. When we passed Skook's camp, we could see him rolled up in his eider-down underneath the tarp. Immediately we started up a steep slope, which soon became a more moderate grade. We climbed steadily. The trees became more stunted and sparse as we approached the timberline. Dawn broke out early at this altitude and we had no difficulty walking on the crust of the snow. It was truly magnificent! The air was crisp and bracing and, when the sun came over the northeastern horizon, the scene was almost beyond human description.

We had not had breakfast, but that did not worry us. Plenty of time to eat, once we were over the other side of the mountain. The trail had long since disappeared under the snowcap, and we had to use the sun to guide us in a northerly direction. Soon we picked up fresh dog-sled runner tracks, which made it easy. All we had to do was follow them and they would lead us to the trail where it emerged on the opposite side of Baldy. We were elated with our discovery and made good time. Our packs were much lighter than when we had left Vanderhoof, and the walking was the best we had experienced since leaving home.

Home! It seemed ages since our departure. Here we were in what appeared to be another world. A vast, white, glistening world just above timberline. Only the occasional stunted balsam managed to keep a precarious foothold here. For several hours we walked, always keeping the runner tracks in sight. Before we realized it, we started down the opposite slope of the mountain. Gradually the trees became more plentiful and taller. Under the largest balsams, the snow began to disappear. Suddenly, two steep downgrades made the descent very fast, and it was not long after passing them that we were again walking on bare ground. It was now around eight a.m. We selected a suitable campsite and ate breakfast.

We had made it! What a break we had received to get a frost like that after rain the day before. Looking back, it seems like a miracle yet, at the same time, we did not think too much about it. After a breakfast of hardtack and boiled raisins, washed down by black tea, we shouldered our packs and started on the last lap of our hike. We estimated that we had between five and six miles to go before reaching the mine.

The trail was still downgrade because we had not yet reached the foot of the mountain. Soon we could hear the rushing waters of a large creek ahead of us. We descended the last grade. There was the creek we had journeyed so far to see — Manson Creek!

We stood on the bank and watched the swollen waters race past. So this was the creek thousands of goldseekers in the 1870's had braved so much to reach. Little did we think then that we might be in the fore of a second rush, but such was the case. We walked a few yards further along the trail and there, for the second time, we saw a grave.

It was at the foot of a small hill. Unlike the one of Hugh Gillis, this one had a little white headboard and fence around it. Obviously someone had recently fixed it up. In black painted letters was the inscription, "Jack Roberts. Died 1872." Much later we found out that this man had been killed a few yards from where he was buried. In 1871, a crude sawmill had been built on the bank of Manson Creek. It was at this mill that the man had met his death.

The trail followed along the edge of the creek for about half a mile, then veered away. Again we started to climb. It was a little frustrating because we thought we had finished with the steep grades after crossing Baldy. Eventually we reached the top, and there we found a fork in the trail. Which one to take became the problem. Both looked little used because only recently had the winter's snow disappeared and because no fresh tracks had been made since. We decided to take the trail to the left, which proved to be the correct one. We suddenly started to descend a very steep hill. About halfway down we could see the valley floor below. There was the mine!

It was built on a sidehill. We could see white steam issuing from some exhaust and wood smoke from the power plant's smokestack. To the left were several buildings of various sizes and beyond them other small buildings which were living quarters for the crew. The sight below us was the end of our long journey. It came as something of an anti-climax. We had got so used to hiking along the trail that it was hard to realize this was where it stopped. We descended to the bottom of the valley known as Slate Creek.

Ogilvie

On our arrival, we were met by three menacing, growling dogs. They had shot from the open doorway of a cabin on the left and ran at us as if they meant to tear us to pieces. A fairly tall, sparely-built man appeared at the doorway and called off his dogs. They quickly obeyed his commands.

He asked us to come in. We had met "Billy" Steele! Billy, as he was known to everyone, quickly made us some fresh tea and, as we talked, was whipping up the dough to make baking powder biscuits. When baked, he set these before us, along with a dish of butter and a can of jam. After the meals we had recently been having of hardtack and raisins, the biscuits seemed like manna from heaven. Bill and I really gorged and Billy kept urging us to eat more. Then, when replete, he offered his can of tobacco and "rollings" and we gratefully accepted, although neither of us was addicted to tobacco.

We told Billy who we were and why we were here. There was no doubt that he was genuinely glad to have company. He told us he had kept a daily diary for many years and that our names would be entered on the day we arrived. He claimed to have come to Manson in 1896, and during the elapsed years had only made a couple of trips "outside." That Billy was a well-educated man there was no doubt. He mentioned that Victoria was his birthplace. (Years later, by sheer accident I met his brother, a retired ship's captain, in Victoria and had lunch with him. He had never seen Billy after he left home for Manson Creek. They were destined never to meet again in this life.)

Billy was a talkative, pleasant man and his anecdotes of his life in the north were most interesting. He showed us peculiar gold nuggets he had collected over the years and also nuggets of native silver and arquerite. The latter is an amalgam of silver and quicksilver or mercury and is not very common.

One of the stories he told us was how four men had died after eating what they thought were mushrooms. He said they were buried on a gravel bench below Discovery Bar, quite close to the creek.

Bill and I did not think too much about it, until about a year or so later. We and two other fellows were tracing an old buried channel across country when we accidentally stumbled upon these graves. The base of the wooden headboards had rotted, but two had fallen with the face down so we could read the carved names.

One fellow, named Shaw, came from New York City and had died on August 8, 1871. The other was named Cook and he came from Hereford, England. He had died the day after Shaw. We were unable to decipher the names on the other boards.

The time passed quickly in his fascinating company, and we would have preferred to stay longer, but had to see about getting a job at the mine. That Billy was a lonely man was plain to see, but it puzzled us. We knew there must be many men at the mine. We were to find the answer shortly.

Only when we asked the name of the boss at the mine did Billy's expression change. He answered abruptly, "Ogilvie." We sensed his hostility and knew he did not like to use the name, so asked nothing further. Bidding him "good day" and again thanking him for his hospitality, we walked the remaining few hundred yards to the mine.

As we approached the building we met a grey-haired workman and asked him where we might find the foreman. He gave us the information and told us his name was Fred Burton. We came to four workmen digging some kind of an excavation. One man, obviously the foreman, was overseeing the job. I approached him and asked, "Are you Mr. Burton?" "Yes," he replied. "Are you hiring any more men to work at the mine?" "I cannot tell you. Mr. Ogilvie does the hiring," was his reply. As an afterthought, he added "You will probably find him at the office near the cookhouse or on the airfield." We thanked him, then reversed direction and went to look for Mr. Ogilvie.

As we neared the cookhouse two men were talking on the road. One was quite a large man, who appeared to need the walking stick he had, and the other was an extremely short, thin man dressed in a blue serge suit, white shirt, and necktie, wearing a snap-brim felt hat.

Being the elder partner, I usually did the talking. On approaching them, I addressed myself to the large man. "Excuse me, but can you tell us where we can find Mr. Ogilvie?" In a very British accent he replied, "Why yes, this is Mr. Ogilvie here," indicating the small man. Both Bill and I were only of medium height, but the small man had to look up at us. "What do you want?" he asked very brusquely. "Are you hiring any more men to work at the mine?" I answered. "Where are you from?" he wanted to know. "Chilco," Bill said. "Where's that?" he asked next. "About thirteen miles northeast of Vanderhoof," I said. "No! I have no work for you," he said in a tone of finality.

It seemed to take a few seconds for this news to sink in, and both Bill and I stood there saying nothing. Then I asked, "Can we purchase enough food to get back to Fort St. James?" "I can give you nothing," replied Ogilvie. This unpleasant little man was beginning to get under my skin. I could feel my face start to flush as I replied, "Mr. Ogilvie, I did not ask you to *give* us anything. I asked if we could purchase some food for the trip out." "We are not running a commissary here," he replied. With that he turned and walked away, the big man with the stick limping alongside.

"Whew! What a stinker," I thought. "The little son of a bitch," was Bill's comment.

That was that! All our dreams of a job and making a stake were shattered in just a few minutes. All the miles of that tough trek for nothing, and it was just as many miles back. What to do about it needed thinking out.

We walked to where an attempt had been made to clear an airstrip beyond the mine. A large boulder had been dragged to one side, and we both sat on it. We were silent — each with his thoughts. The talk with Ogilvie had unsettled me. For some reason, he seemed to positively dislike us. What had we done? It was no crime to ask for employment. Even if no work was available, he did not have to be so unpleasant about it. These thoughts kept going through my mind, but I could find no solution.

We must have sat there an hour or more when Bill suddenly said, "I'll bet Billy will sell us enough grub to get out." That was it! Billy Steele would help us, we were sure, and we both began to feel better. In fact, we began to take an interest in what was around us.

Why were they making this airstrip? We had seen no planes land at Fort St. James. It looked extremely short to us. It turned out it was short. After it was finished a plane attempted to land and cracked up.

Bill, who sat facing towards the mine, turned his head to me and said, "Here's that little son of a bitch again. I suppose he does not want me to sit on his damned rock. Well, just let him try to remove me."

I turned to look. Sure enough, Ogilvie was approaching us, and we both thought he was going to order us to get going. Ogilvie stopped a few feet from us and neither of us attempted to get up. I guess he knew just what we thought of him. He spoke. His tone, though not friendly, was nevertheless different from the way he had spoken before. "I'll make a deal with you fellows. In three days time we are going with the 'cat' and trailer to break a trail over Baldy. If you will give us a hand over the hump, I'll give you enough grub to take you back to the Fort. In the meantime you can work a couple of days or so around the mine. Is it a deal?" "It's a deal!" I said, after a pause. Bill nodded agreement. "Very well. Take your bedrolls and see Mr. Burroughs. He will tell you where to sleep," he said. With that he turned and hurried away, as if he could not bear to converse with common mortals a minute longer than was necessary.

We sat a few more minutes and watched him disappear. Then getting up, threw on our packs, and went looking for Mr. Burroughs, whoever he might be. As we approached the cookhouse, the big man with the walking stick was on the road. When a few feet from him, he said, "I am Burroughs. Mr. Ogilvie told me you would be coming. I'll show you to your cabin where you can sleep." He led us to a shack with four wooden pole beds in it, but the mattresses were good. There was no one else there. On leaving he told us breakfast would be at seven sharp. He seemed a decent chap and we wondered how he could stand working under Ogilvie.

After a good wash and shave we felt better, and after supper went over to visit our new friend Billy Steele. Billy was alone, except for his dogs, which again dashed out at us. One word from Billy and they were quiet. We told him what had happened and Billy nodded. "Yes," he said, "Ogilvie would pull some kind of a deal like that. You will earn your grub, you can be sure of that." How true and prophetic were his words! We stayed and talked for a long time, because his stories of the earlier days fascinated us.

Before leaving we asked why the men at the mine did not come over and visit with him. Billy laughed and said they were probably scared to lose their jobs. He and Ogilvie did not get along because he was living on what was now C. M. & S. property, which had formerly been staked by Ogilvie. He told them he intended to stay, because he had been in that cabin long before the C. M. & S. or Ogilvie came into the country. Billy had openly criticized Ogilvie's mining methods and told him he did not know what he was doing. His statement had a lot of truth in it. Evidently someone had goofed badly on drainage engineering.

Bill and I, of course, knew nothing about mining at that time. As we gained experience in several types of placer mining, we came to realize just how poorly laid out the whole of the Slate Creek operation of the C. M. & S. was. It was a slack-line type of operation. That is, at one end was the power plant — in this case an upright steam engine — at the other end an anchored tower supported by guy lines. In between the two, the bucket cables were stretched. The idea being to lower the bucket into the pit and bring it up full of gravel or "paydirt," as it is called, by the steam hoist.

Once it is hoisted to the top of the washing plant the bucket is tilted and the gravel is dumped on to what is known as a "grizzly." This consists of a number of steel rails with sufficient space between them to allow the smaller gravels to fall through to a hopper beneath. The gravel is then washed through the sluice boxes where the gold and other heavy concentrates are trapped in the riffles. The larger boulders stay on the "grizzly" bars and are washed by forced jets of water to clear them of any possible paydirt sticking to them. They are then dumped on an endless belt, which takes them away from the washing plant and leaves them in a heap, something like a pyramid.

This type of mining has several serious drawbacks, even under the best of conditions. First, the whole set-up is limited by the length of cable between the power plant and the anchor. At Slate Creek it was further complicated by the bucket having to dig under approximately ten feet of water and among some very large boulders. A drainage ditch had been built to the pit, but it had not been started sufficiently downstream to drain the pit of water. As a result the bucket was always digging "blind." The pit could be freed of most of the water by using additional pumping equipment, but it was a poor substitute for a natural bedrock drain. In addition to this, by using a fixed type of power plant, the tailings were having to be dumped on "virgin" ground — that is, ground that had not been worked for gold before the thousands of tons of gravel were dumped on it.

It is hard to know why one of the largest and richest mining companies in the world, with some of the best mining engineers, used this type of operation which could not possibly succeed. It did not operate for long. After a few years it closed down and has not been reopened since. (According to the magazine *Western Miner*, the mine's production in gold was a little more than $17,000 the first year and $36,000 the second.)

After Bill and I left Billy Steele's that night, we returned to our sleeping quarters and turned in to rest for the day ahead. We were up early because we did not want to miss breakfast. Ogilvie, despite everything, ran a good cookhouse. The food was excellent and both of us, after our short rations on the trail, did full justice to the breakfast. We were the last to leave the table.

At eight o'clock Mr. Burton told us to accompany him, and he put us to work with pick and shovel. We had to excavate a hole eight feet long by four feet wide and six feet deep. It looked like a slightly oversize grave. Bill and I jokingly asked each other whether we were going to be buried in it after Ogilvie got through with us. It was not easy work because the ground was full of boulders, but we were working and getting paid for it, which is what we hoped to do when we left home. Every half hour or so Mr. Burton would come to see what progress we were making. He was not a bad fellow, but of a nervous type. He appeared to be scared of his job and forever looking to see if Ogilvie was around. Well, jobs as foremen were not easily come by, and he probably had a wife and family to support besides.

Time quickly passed and the steam whistle at twelve o'clock noon told us it was lunchtime. We were walking swiftly towards camp, when we caught up to the two Mikes, whom we had left in the little cabin on the other side of Baldy. It was still freezing at higher altitudes at night, so they had walked over the hump on the snow crust that morning. Down here in the Slate Creek Valley it was warm and sunny. The two Mikes walked with us into camp. On the way we told them we had no luck as far as steady employment was concerned, and that we were to leave again in a few days to break a trail over Baldy, with the cat. Before entering the cookhouse for lunch, we said we would see them again when we had finished work for the day.

After supper we joined them. They had eaten at the cookhouse, too. Imagine our surprise when they told us Ogilvie had hired them to work at the mine. Mike Zalitach was to fire the boiler and from then on was known to everyone as "Boiler" Mike. His partner who was to work up on the grizzly was naturally called "Grizzly" Mike. The nicknames acquired at the C. M. & S. mine on Slate Creek stayed with them the rest of their lives.

The following day four more fellows walked over the Baldy snow-cap, because the weather was still clear, with frost at high altitude. They did not get steady work. Ogilvie made them the same proposition he had put to us, the only difference being they got two days work at the mine. Two of the fellows, Gus Sabo and Steve Firko, were Hungarians, but they had not been as lucky as their fellow countrymen, the two Mikes. Another was a Canadian boy from southern British Columbia, and the last was a short, stocky French Canadian from Montreal, with the inevitable nickname of "Frenchy." He had had an extremely tough time making the trip from Vanderhoof, having nothing to eat but a handful of raisins, washed down by cold water each day of his journey. He had absolutely nothing on his pack except one threadbare blanket when he arrived at Slate Creek.

Poor Frenchy really gorged himself on his first meal at the cookhouse, and he paid for it afterwards. He had been so short of food so long that his stomach revolted when he ate so much. He suffered terrible cramps and was in agony until he finally vomited, which brought him relief. That evening the flunkey brought him some canned milk thinned down by water and what appeared to be soda biscuits. He suffered no after effects and next morning ate a light breakfast of cereal, toast, and one boiled egg. He was fine after that and did he ever lay away the grub at every meal.

Frenchy, Steve, Gus, and the boy from southern British Columbia, whose name was White, now joined Bill and me on another excavation project. This one was approximately sixteen feet square and about five feet deep. Evidently it was for the foundation of a tower. The excavation was so large that all six of us had no difficulty working on it together. The weather was beautiful and we peeled down to the waist when working. The days passed quickly and each evening Bill and I, now accompanied by Les White, would call on Billy Steele. On each visit he would recount something new, often referring to his diary and giving us the exact date of the event.

All too soon came the inevitable morning of our departure. The cat and a wheeled trailer were all set, and about ten a.m., Mr.

Burroughs brought us the pay cheques for the work we had done at the mine. Bill and I received seven dollars and fifty cents each, and the others five dollars because they had worked a day less. Two-fifty a day and free board! Boy! A person could really make a stake if he worked all summer and fall at that rate of pay, because the mine operated seven days a week. I felt very saddened when we had to leave. Despite Ogilvie, I liked the country and the other people with whom we had made contact. I personally was determined to return to the Manson Creek area at the earliest opportunity.

The cat and trailer made good time to the foot of Baldy. Besides the driver Fred, Ogilvie came along to show him the route over the snowcap. It was a gasoline driven tractor without a bulldozer blade, but it had a winch at the rear. The trailer reminded me of an over-size farm wagon with very large wheels and a stake body. The gas and oil were in a separate compartment up front, with the food and other gear stowed at the rear. Ogilvie rode on the cat with the driver and the six of us who were to help over the hump climbed aboard the trailer.

Soon we started to climb the steep grades on Baldy. It was hard to believe we were on our way out again. It was only a few days earlier that we passed the now familiar landmarks in the opposite direction on the way to the mine. We were full of hope and optimism then, but now things were not so rosy. Well, at least we had tried!

The snow was getting deeper as we climbed, and soon the tracks began to spin because they were badly worn. We jumped off the trailer and each took a shovel and mattock. However, we did not have to use them yet, because Fred, the driver, unhooked the cat from the trailer and fastened the winch-hook to it. He then went ahead, letting out the winch cable as he did so. Then, finding a more level spot, he started to winch the trailer to the cat. It was slow progress, but worked well enough until the snow got too deep for the cat to climb under its own power.

It was now up to us to get busy with the shovels to dig out enough so the cat was not high-centred — that is, so the snow under the cat between the tracks did not prevent the cat from sinking down to get good footing. The mattock had to be used to break the crust on the snow before we could dig. The six of us were strung out in a line on the steep grades digging a trench so the body of the cat would not drag. It was hard, hot work, on a sunny and warm day. About three o'clock we had lunch consisting of sandwiches prepared at the cookhouse before we left the mine. The driver had built a fire and made a big pail of tea. We were sure ready for it because breakfast had been at seven that morning. Ogilvie sat alone to one side, not saying a word to anyone.

All that afternoon we made tedious progress in the same manner. The cat would straddle our trench, then when at the limit of the cable, would winch the trailer to it. Late that evening we came to the last steep grade before the summit levelled off at timberline. We had to dig every inch of that grade. Bill and I were up front and worked until almost dark, which meant about eleven p.m. at that altitude near the end of May.

We were all in, so tired we stumbled our way back to where the camp had been made for the night. The others had returned before us and were eating around a big fire. We loaded our tin plates with sausages and beans and filled the mugs with tea. I emptied two before eating, such thirsty work had been the snow shovelling. Fred had cut lots of balsam boughs for the beds, so it did not take us long to prepare our blankets. Besides being the driver of the cat, he also did most of the cooking and making camp. We saw no sign of Ogilvie and presumed he was sleeping on the trailer.

At seven the next morning we had eaten breakfast and were on our way. We could easily walk on the snow crust as there had been more frost during the night. The cat had no trouble following the trench up the steep grade to the summit and winching up the trailer. Ogilvie was now walking ahead probing the snow with a steel-tipped pole, finding where the snow was shallowest and searching for any hidden potholes.

The day was absolutely cloudless and the sun extremely dazzling on the snow, which on the summit averaged around two and a half feet. The high winds had prevented it piling up during the winter. However, the depressions were all levelled off and had to be avoided by the cat. There could be twenty or more feet of snow in them, depending on their depth. It was extremely slow because the route had to be probed continuously. We did not have to dig unless we came to a shallow depression which could not be avoided. We stopped and ate at noon. Both Ogilvie and the driver wore sunglasses, but we had none. We did not know enough to blacken around the eyes with charcoal. This would have helped cut down the dazzling glare from the snow. Evening found us still on the summit and only about half way from the foot of Baldy. However, we

43

would soon be on the downgrade and we should be able to make better time if all went well. After supper the six of us sat talking around the fire of cordwood brought from the mine on the trailer, because there was no firewood available where we were.

The two Hungarians, Steve and Gus, said if it froze enough they were going to leave Ogilvie at dawn, because already we had spent two days travelling about six miles from the foot of the mountain. They did not have much grub, but had cached some from each meal we had eaten since starting from Slate Creek and figured that would last them until they reached Fort St. James. They had been thinking ahead. That had never occurred to us! Actually, they could not be blamed. There was no pay for this trip, only grub to get us back to the Fort. Besides, we were all suffering from partial snow-blindness and inflamed eyes. Bill, my partner, appeared in the worst shape. The reflected sunlight seemed to irritate his eyes the most making them extremely red and bloodshot. The only medication we had was cold tea, which helped alleviate the soreness.

We did not sleep much that night — at least five of us didn't. Only Frenchy slept well. Nothing seemed to bother him now that there was plenty of grub to be had.

True to their previous statements, Steve and Gus packed up their bedrolls at three a.m. and left, because there was a slight frost. I was sorry to see them leave. It would probably mean more work for the four of us who were left.

We did not stay out of any sense of loyalty towards Ogilvie — he was not the type to inspire it in the average man. He was the most aloof and egotistical person I had ever encountered anywhere. Why he was that way is not easy to fathom. Perhaps his small stature made him sensitive and he enjoyed his role as an employer of labour, with the power it carried over bigger men. Or perhaps it was because his father was the first governor of the Yukon. I don't pretend to know the answer. The only reason we stayed is that we were out of grub, and Ogilvie knew it, too.

By six o'clock we were eating breakfast on the third day since leaving the mine. Fred had told us he hoped to reach the foot of Baldy on the opposite side by evening. It was still cloudless, so we knew we would get another day of sun glare from the snow unless we descended to the timber belt very quickly.

It did not work out that way. We ran into difficulties soon after setting out. The cat slid into a buried ravine and was lying almost on its side — the snow had collapsed under it. To make things worse, water to a depth of two feet was at the bottom. Fortunately the trailer was not attached at the time, because the trail was being broken ahead of it. At first glance it looked a hopeless situation to get out of, but by hard work and ingenuity, the cat was righted and in reverse gear backed out, using the winch and tracks together. We shovelled a small mountain of snow and in the process got soaked to the waist from the slush in the bottom.

It was a poor start. We had lost almost two and a half hours. Nevertheless, we were glad to see the cat forging ahead again. Ogilvie was still probing the snow, and we used the long handles of the shovels as probes, and worked on both sides of him. No one wanted to see the cat take another nose dive into some buried hole.

The glare from the snow was terrific, and it was not long before our eyes were burning and sore again. Mine felt as if they were full of sand particles and got worse as the day wore on. Bill really suffered. In addition, his nose and face were almost beet-red from sunburn. He was fair-complexioned and, even at the best of times, could not suntan the way most men do when exposed to ultraviolet rays. On our way in we had enjoyed the hike over the snowcap, but this return trip was something else. Hour after hour of that long day we inched our way along, the cat breaking the trail after we had probed it, then winching the trailer to it, only to continuously repeat the process. We ate a cold lunch — no one wanted to waste any more time after our disastrous start.

Around four o'clock in the afternoon we started downgrade and we could see the timbered valley below. It was a cheering sight. We still had to probe the snow, but now the cat could pull the trailer without winching. We made much better time. About an hour later we entered the timbered belt, and the snow became heavy and soft, only about a foot deep. The cat and trailer were making fast time, and we had to walk hard to keep up, because now we were behind.

Every few minutes the tracks on the cat would crack, almost like rifle shots, because the wet snow was balling up between the drive sprockets and the tracks. Suddenly it happened! The cat threw one of its tracks! I think we all felt a little sick at the stomach. Here we were so close to the end of the snow belt and the foot of the mountain, only to have this happen. Fortunately the track was not broken, it had only jumped the drive sprocket and front idlers.

45

Fred grabbed an axe and cut down a small tree of about six-inch diameter, which he then topped at about half that size. This made a stout pry something like sixteen feet long. He explained just how he wanted us to use this as a fulcrum, using the butts of other trees to exert terrific pressure on the side of the track as he slowly moved the machine. It worked beautifully and it was not long before the track was back in position. We were moving again!

Soon bare ground began to appear, then finally we left the snow behind completely. We reached the foot of the mountain about nine o'clock that night. Bill could see nothing as his eyes hurt him so much, and to me the firelight seemed a peculiar greenish colour. I brought him a little food to eat. He had no appetite, but he drank plenty of hot tea, as did we all. We bathed our eyes in the tea which was left in the pail after it had cooled, and it gave us much relief from the soreness. After making a good big bed of balsam boughs, we turned in. May 31, 1935 was a day we would remember as long as we lived.

Return to "The Fort"

We were up early the next morning — this was the day we were to part company with Ogilvie and his cat. They were to pick up the supplies which Skookum Davidson had brought in by pack train some time previously and return to the mine. They would have no difficulty now the trail was broken, providing there was no mechanical failure.

The dog team had taken some of the more essentials further up the mountain, but the heavy loads of food and equipment were piled beneath a big tarp under some spruce trees.

We had finished breakfast and had our beds rolled, ready to place on the pack-boards, when Ogilvie came across to the four of us. "You fellows follow me," he said. Then, turning around, he strode away without a backward glance to see if we were following. He had to play the "big boss" to the very last minute.

Frenchy, Les, Bill, and I walked to where he was standing, near a cache of supplies. Spread on a tarp was a good variety of food-stuffs. "Well, there you are! Help yourself!" he exclaimed, then walked over to the driver who was loading the trailer.

Frenchy had come prepared. He had a gunny sack with him, procured somehow off the trailer. He loaded it with everything in sight. It was so full he could not tie the neck of it with a piece of twine, so he reluctantly discarded one of his four-pound tins of jam. Poor Frenchy! He did not mean to go hungry on the trip out.

We filled our arms with sufficient food to last each of us five or six days because we did not want to burden ourselves with excessive weight. We loaded our packs and helped Frenchy with his, estimating the total weight to be about one hundred pounds. Considering he had only one thin blanket and a pack-board, he must have had better than ninety pounds of food.

We sure got a big kick out of him because he was a likeable fellow and very lively company. It was fearful the way he could murder the English language. Life would have been pretty grim in those days without a few Frenchy's around.

Turning our faces south to Fort St. James, we started out on the long trail back. We wished Fred a good return trip and he wished us good luck on ours. Ogilvie was nowhere in sight and we figured we had seen the last of him, but it did not work out that way. Our next meeting did nothing to enhance him in our eyes.

It soon became apparent that Frenchy could not keep up the pace, so heavily burdened was he by his pack. He had to rest quite frequently, so he told us to go ahead and he would see us in Fort St. James eventually. We did not like to leave him, but he insisted he would be all right and that he would eat his way back to the Fort. We had no alternative. We did not have the food to eat our way back. A turn in the trail soon lost him to view, because we were making a good pace. The fine weather had dried many of the wet spots and the walking on the whole was much better than when we came in.

Les was a good companion for Bill and me — he was much like us in our outlook on life. His chief ambition was to earn enough money to be an airline pilot. He had a good physique, being a non-drinker or smoker.

By noon we had reached Gillis' Grave and ate lunch at the first creek we came to after passing it. Evening found us at the cabins where we had first encountered Fred Smith and Alex Kynoch. It was a pleasant spot to stay, and after a leisurely supper we relaxed and tried to plan something for the future, once we were back in civilization. As usual, it seemed as if we were up against a brick wall, now that our hopes of steady work had been shattered at Slate Creek.

Les said he would head for his home town of Chilliwack if there was no sign other employment might be found around Fort St. James.

Bill and I still hoped to try gold mining on our own sometime, but it seemed out of the question at present on the few dollars we had. It would require more money than we could raise to grubstake ourselves and hire a packer to take it over the trail to Manson Creek. Flying in supplies would be the quickest way, but the cost was around eleven cents a pound.

However, we were confident we could grubstake ourselves for a summer in Manson Creek for much less than the two hundred dollars we had previously been told it would cost. Food was cheap and, by taking only the essentials of flour, beans, rice, salt, tea, etc., it should not cost too much. Our rifles would be taken along to provide us with fresh meat and game birds. We were in an optimistic mood as we turned in for the night.

Another sparkling morning found us getting up about seven-thirty, after treating ourselves to the luxury of an extra hour or so in bed. There was nothing to hurry over — we were just three of the thousands of unemployed with plenty of time to spare!

While eating breakfast we fell to discussing how far back on the trail Frenchy might be. Bill remarked that he hoped a grizzly bear had not met up with him. Les laughed and said, "Not a chance of that. I feel sorry for any grizzly that tries to take the grub away from Frenchy." However, I felt a little uneasy because we had left Frenchy behind. The others felt the same way, so we decided to stay at the cabin and wait for him to catch up. We could divide his excess grub and put it on our own packs. That way he would be able to keep up with us.

We spent a happy, relaxed day at the cabin, which gave us an opportunity to bathe, shave, and change some of our clothing. Having only toilet soap for clothes washing was not too efficient, but at least after they had been washed in hot water, then rinsed in the cold mountain creek, they were much improved. We dried them outside because the day was sunny and warm.

Our eyes too, were almost normal again after the terrible sun-glare on the Baldy snowcap. Bill's eyes were still red, but most of the soreness had gone. Each of us continued to use the cold tea after each meal for eye irritation. About four that afternoon little Frenchy came plodding along under his heavy pack. We were happy to see him join us again, and he was just as relieved to throw off his pack and rest.

After a bite to eat and several mugs of coffee, which he preferred to tea, he was just as lively as ever. Much to our delight he immediately started again to tear apart the English language; as he told of various adventures of his in Quebec.

We all felt much better for our stay at Twelve Mile Cabins, but now the time had come to once more shoulder our packs and continue the trek back to Fort St. James. All that day we walked at a steady pace, stopping only for the noon meal and our usual rest periods.

It was late in the afternoon when we overtook a trapper and his wife, who were making a very leisurely pace travelling the same direction as we. They were accompanied by two large pack dogs, which were so heavily packed they actually rolled from side to side with each step. The dogs were a few feet to the rear of the people and they paid not the slightest attention to us when we passed them.

As we caught up to the couple, the man turned and greeted us with the familiar "Hi!" He was of medium height and build, but his wife was not quite so ordinary. Larger than the average, she was very well-built, with wide Slavic features topped by a mass of real blonde "bobbed" hair.

We did not know it at the time we met them, but it was one of their trapline cabins that Bill and I had used on the trip in to Manson, when we had slept on the caribou hides. This, then, was how we first met Louie Kohse and his wife. Returning the man's salute, we passed them, for they were travelling at a much slower pace owing to the heavily laden dogs.

Soon we started thinking about supper and a place to camp for the night, although there were several hours of daylight left. We picked out a suitable place beside a small creek and spruce thicket, and proceeded to make our beds. It had been a good day's hike. We estimated we had made at least thirty miles. The trail was drying rapidly after the run-off, and it was hard to imagine we had encountered so much water on the way in. Actually, there was much natural gravel, and once the frozen ground had thawed, the water simply drained through it.

We had just finished our meal when we heard voices. It was the couple we had passed who, with their dogs, had now caught up to us. They, too, decided to camp near the creek for the night, about fifty yards upstream from us. We watched them take the packs off the dogs. Once they were free of their burdens, they immediately rolled on their backs among the pine needles. Snorting and blowing, they would stand up, shake themselves, then roll over and repeat the performance again and again. I had seen pack horses do it after being relieved of their loads and now knew dogs did exactly the same.

After the man had prepared a bed, he came over to talk to us while his wife was cooking supper. We told him why we had gone to Manson Creek and about our return trip over Baldy, with its hardships. He told us both he and his brother had traplines in the Klawli country, and that it was at his brother's cabin we had stayed to rest up for a few days. He said we were now camped at a place called "Giddigingla" and should have no trouble making it to Fort

St. James in a couple of days. He planned on a longer time owing to the heavy packs. We presumed they must be taking out some of their winter's catch of furs, although he did not say so.

The four of us broke camp early next morning and were on our way after a good meal of flapjacks, which Frenchy had made. We still had quite a bit left of "Ogilvie's grub," as we called it.

The weather was good and so far no mosquitoes had bothered us, although we knew by this time there would be millions at Chilco. By suppertime that evening we were back at Tsilcoh Creek, where Bill and I had rested our blistered feet on the way up. We decided to camp there because we knew it was less than twenty miles to Fort St. James, which we could easily make the next day. We were up fairly early the next morning, knowing we were close to the Fort. We were anxious to arrive there, although I don't think any one of us could have given a valid reason for feeling that way, because there was no work to be obtained there.

It was a little more than a mile of travel until we saw the straight, seemingly endless road of Juniper Straight stretching ahead of us. It was here where Bill and I, on the way up, had such an exhausting experience in the gumbo and water. Once we had descended to a lower level we were back in the same muck again.

True, the water had subsided quite a lot, but the mud was as sticky as ever and seemed bottomless. There was nothing to do but walk into it, if "walk" is the right word. "Stagger" would be more appropriate. We were very relieved to find the worst stretch was only about two hundred yards across. The ground beyond was soft, but firm enough to take our weight if we were careful. Gradually the roadbed improved until it was quite hard and we made good time. Soon we came to a wagon branch road from Juniper Straight, and here we found about twenty natives — men, women, and children — camped. After the usual greetings, one of the men told us they were waiting for Perison's truck to pick them up, the road being passable this far from Fort St. James.

The natives had come in from a place called Pinchi, which we gathered was some twenty miles west on the wagon road. Evidently they had been camped here overnight to await the arrival of the truck. We decided to push on to the Fort, because it was uncertain what time of day the truck was supposed to arrive. We had walked more than a mile when we saw the truck travelling towards us several miles away on the flat and straight road.

We sat down on a windfall and awaited its arrival. The vehicle stopped opposite us and a big man hailed us from the cab. It was Harold Perison himself driving, and with him a big "swamper." We exchanged greetings (as everyone did in those days) and after the usual queries regarding our trek, Harold told us to jump on the deck of the truck. He was going right back to Fort St. James once he had picked up the natives. Well, Bill and I had started the trip to Manson Creek by riding in a car for the first four miles or so, and here we were returning the last sixteen miles to Fort St. James on the back of a truck.

We made good time and, though the road was rutty and rough, were soon back in the Fort. Harold dropped us off in front of his home. We told him we had very little money, but we would work to pay for the lift. He said he did not want anything from us for the ride. If we wished, we could give him a hand to buzz up some cordwood. After a hurried meal, he started the engine on the buzz saw and the four of us soon had the cordwood reduced to blocks of firewood. After this little job was completed, we had to decide where we were going to stay and also discuss any plans we might have for the future. It seemed as if Bill and I had again run up against the usual dead end.

Shouldering our packs, we walked down to the camping ground along the creek. More men than ever were there, and we could not find an empty camp. We talked with many of them and discussed our trip to Manson. Some were deciding to go there, and they were very anxious to find out everything they could. We could not give them much information, other than the road conditions and what the mining operation on Slate Creek was doing. We knew nothing about the Manson Creek "diggings" at all.

Someone informed us there were some empty cabins for rent on "Huffman's Point," a gravel beach on Stuart Lake. The four of us — Frenchy, Les, Bill and I — walked over there. We had a few dollars between us, although Frenchy had none as we had not yet cashed the C. M. & S. cheques. Les had the most. There was an empty log cabin and a few frame cabins, and we could see at least one of them was occupied.

Les decided he would like to rent the log cabin, if the cost was not too much. He wanted to stay in the Fort for a time, and if no job came his way he was going to return home. We went to see Mrs.

Huffman, the owner of the cabin, who said the rent was four dollars a month and that we would have to supply our own firewood.

Les paid her a month in advance, so she came over and unlocked it for us. It was plainly but adequately furnished, three cots with straw mattresses, cookstove, table, and four chairs. In one corner was a washstand and hanging on the wall, a coal oil lamp. One of us would have to sleep on the floor, but that was no hardship. Frenchy, Bill, and I flipped coins to see who would take the two beds. Les was entitled to his, seeing he had paid the rent. The odd man out had to sleep on the floor. On the first flip, all the coins finished tails up, so we flipped a second time. This time Bill's coin was tails, ours were heads, which meant Bill had the floor.

After breakfast next morning, we all decided to have a look at the settlement of Fort St. James. It was not a large place and seemed to consist of one main street. Frame and log houses were set in small clearings with the trees almost to the back doors. However, as we walked further, the Hudson's Bay store and buildings were in a large, open clearing overlooking Stuart Lake. Beyond this property was a large reservation. Many men sat in front of the store on this warm, sunny day.

After awhile Bill and I decided to have a look around inside, thinking we might buy a few small articles, although it was vital we should conserve our meagre supply of cash. Inside the door stood a young fellow who had obviously just arrived — his pack-board with bedroll was propped at his feet. We spoke to him and he told us he hoped to find a job somewhere around the Fort. We laughed and told him we, along with a hundred others, had the same idea. Yet it was while talking with him that one of the most amazing and inexplicable incidents occurred.

Who should enter the door but Ogilvie, with whom we had parted company at the foot of Baldy. It was obvious he had returned to Slate Creek and had flown out by plane to Fort St. James. Dressed as always in his tight-fitting suit, with a snap-brim felt hat pulled well down over his eyes, he walked past everyone to the manager's office and closed the door. As he passed the thought suddenly flashed through my mind that I had never seen this man without a hat, despite the fact we had been several days in his company after leaving Slate Creek. I wondered idly if he was bald.

A few minutes later the door of the office opened, and he walked toward the store entrance where we were still standing. He stopped in front of us and, completely ignoring Bill and me, addressed himself to the young fellow whose name was Bud. He asked, "You just arrived?" Bud answered, "Yes." "Do you want a job?" "Sure!" Bud replied. "All right," said Ogilvie, "There is a plane leaving for Manson Creek in an hour's time. Tell the pilot Mr. Ogilvie sent you, and he will take you." With that, he walked outside.

Bill and I were speechless! It was inexplicable! Here the two of us had hiked one hundred and twenty miles with heavy packs, under adverse conditions, to try and find employment with this man, only to be refused. Now he had hired a stranger under our very noses. We could only presume he did it for his own satisfaction. He could have hired any one of the dozen men outside the store, had he really wanted a man. An insufferable little stuffed shirt!

The three of us walked back to Huffman's Point, because it was here Bud was supposed to catch the plane. We left him there and entered the cabin. Les and Frenchy were back and had returned with Steve and Gus, who had left Ogilvie on the trip over Baldy. They were camped in an abandoned log cabin somewhere just off the highway, and like us had no plans for the future. Frenchy told us he was leaving the next day for Vanderhoof, because he had the chance to ride on a truck. He was hoping he might find a job with a farmer somewhere around there. Poor, happy-go-lucky Frenchy! Many times I have wondered where he went and how he fared — and if he ever returned to his native Quebec. We never saw him again.

The next day, after we had seen Frenchy depart, we met the big swamper who had been riding with Perison in the truck on the north road. His name was Tommy Ahyee and he offered to take us around and tell us anything we wanted to know about the Fort. Tommy, who was a half-breed, volunteered the information that there was to be a dance on the reservation that night and asked would we like to go? We said we might, if it was permissible, which he assured us it was. Tommy told us quite a bit about the "Fort," as everyone called it.

It was founded in 1806, and at one time was the seat of government for the whole of New Caledonia, long before the province of British Columbia came into existence. The two most famous figures of its history, without a doubt, were James Douglas and Kwah, the Carrier chief who spared the life of the other. In so doing, Chief

Kwah altered the whole history of British Columbia. Douglas, who later was knighted, became the first governor of British Columbia.

The Fort saw a mighty gold rush during the years 1870-71, when thousands of men from the Cariboo passed through on their way to Manson and Germansen gold fields. The city of Ogden, Utah, is named after one of the Hudson's Bay factors, buried at the Fort. The story of Fort St. James is colourful and exciting.

On our previous walk through the village we had noticed a neat frame house set a few yards back from the highway. We asked Tommy who lived there and he said an old bachelor prospector named Dave Purvis. Bill and I knew nothing about prospecting, but it sounded interesting, so we decided to call on Dave. We found him to be of medium height and build and of an age around sixty-five. He was very willing to talk to us about his life of roaming the hills in search of a fortune. There were rocks spread out in neat rows in the front room, especially near the windows. Even to our inexperienced eyes we knew many of them contained visible amounts of mineralization.

We spent several enjoyable hours with Dave. Not only had he grouped and classified the rocks, but each of the groups elicited an anecdote about where they came from. One type of rock which was rather unusual was composed of greyish-white material with red stringers through it. When questioned, he explained it was cinnabar. Seeing we did not understand, he told us it was mercury ore. He then went on to tell us it came from the top of a big hill overlooking Pinchi Lake, but at the present time it was not of high enough grade to be of commercial value. None of us realized at the time that we were looking, literally, at a million dollar find. Several years later the famous Pinchi Lake mine opened on the hill where Dave had picked up his one sample.

Two years after he showed us these samples, some government geologists visited the Pinchi Lake area and saw this outcrop of cinnabar, which they reported. One of the geologists was credited with the discovery, but I and many others in Fort St. James knew he was not the original discoverer. It seemed to be one of the ironies of prospecting, in those days, that quite often the man with packsack on his back received nothing, while others received the credit and still others made the money. Nowadays it is not so. The average prospector is well-versed in most phases of mining and knows how to draw up a contract when he finds anything worthwhile.

55

Before taking leave of Dave, we sat around and had coffee with him. We told him we hoped to return to the Manson Creek country sometime and do some prospecting on our own. He cautioned us that all he had received for his years in the hills was the house he lived in. All things considered, it was a healthy, free life, but he added that it was not meant for a married man with a family to support.

Later that evening the three of us decided to look in on the dance held on the Necoslie Reserve. We saw Steve and Gus and they decided to accompany us. Tommy met us at the door, and we sat just inside the building on a long wooden bench. Not many natives were inside, it still being daylight, but more were arriving all the time. The music was supplied by two men, one playing a violin and the other a guitar. The older people seemed content to sit around watching and talking, but the younger ones were having a great time. They seemed to prefer the dances with lots of action, such as one-steps and square dances. It was very similar to any country dance attended by white people. One notable exception was the young native males who kept on their hats when dancing, as was the custom.

Everyone seemed to attend for one reason — to have a good time. No drinking was in evidence anywhere. Around eleven o'clock the Catholic priest came in. He did not seem at all pleased to see us sitting there, but said nothing. We decided to leave soon afterward, because the dance hall was getting very crowded and some had no place to sit.

Bob Dunsmore

The next morning we saw the elderly man who lived in a small frame house near to us. He was on the shingle beach in front, trying to roll a drift log to his sawhorse for bucking into firewood. It was much too heavy for him, so we all went to give him a helping hand to put it in position. Bill then started to saw and I split the blocks into stove wood, which Les packed to the woodbox on the verandah. It did not take long to dispose of the log. He thanked us for helping him.

That was the way we met Bob Dunsmore, and this chance meeting changed the whole pattern of life for Bill and me. We quite naturally talked of our recent trip to Manson, with its disappointments, when Bob surprised us by saying both he and his wife were going in there, although his wife would be along later. He explained they owned a placer lease on Lost Creek and that one of their sons was in there already, waiting for them to come in with a season's supply of grub.

He asked us why we did not join him, if we had money enough to grubstake ourselves and pay the freighter's charges of six cents a pound. We explained we knew nothing about digging gold, but he said they would show us how to set up and even put us on some ground where we had a reasonable chance of making a little money. It sounded like a dream come true to Bill and I. We reasoned if we only made a dollar a day each, we would make more than two hundred dollars between us before fall was ended. We were so excited that night we could barely sleep.

Les said he would stay in the Fort for the time being, but he would return home if nothing showed up. He did not plan on going back to Manson. The following day we caught a ride to Vanderhoof with a freight truck to draw the balance of our tie-making money to buy grub for the trip. As on the first occasion, we bought grub from Breen's Store. It consisted mostly of flour, beans, rice, sugar, with, of course, a little jam, peanut butter, dried milk, lard, etc. Tea was our beverage and we hoped to be able to kill some game for meat, having borrowed a .22 rifle. We loaded the supplies on the truck which was due to return to Fort St. James later in the day. Having some time on our hands before returning, we went to see our friend Chuey and ate a meal in his restaurant.

The truck left Vanderhoof around two p.m. and we arrived back in the Fort in time for supper, because the road — though narrow — was quite good. We unloaded our grub and went over to see Bob Dunsmore. He, too, had bought some supplies, which were stacked just inside the door, and I could not help but notice we seemed to have more than he. He told us he had seen the freighter, who would be there at six sharp the next morning, and that we had better be all packed and ready.

Sure enough, a wagon pulled by six horses drove up in front of Bob's house a few minutes before six o'clock the next day. The driver was one of the toughest looking characters I had ever laid eyes on. A bristle of beard, which stuck straight out, covered most of his face and the battered old Stetson on his head was a marvel to behold. The remainder of his outfit was strictly cowboy and not by any stretch of the imagination could any part of it be called new. Of medium height, wide-shouldered, lithe and quick in his movements, you immediately sensed that here was a man who was as tough as he looked.

A little girl, four or five years of age, still sat in the driver's seat on the wagon, and a few minutes later a slim woman riding a brown horse, dismounted and tied the horse to a nearby tree. Bill and I walked over. It was a surprise to me when the driver greeted us. His voice was quite mild, almost gentle. Throughout the long trip ahead of us he spoke the same way at all times. Never once did we hear him raise his voice in anger or use profanity, yet many things happened which must have tried his patience.

By the time we had put on all the supplies, the wagon was fully loaded. Besides our grub and Bob Dunsmore's supplies, the driver was taking in an amount of goods to trade for gold from the miners and prospectors. In addition, he had to take in oats for feed for the team, plus some pack-saddles to pack the grub to various places where the wagon could not go.

When seven o'clock rolled around we were once again ready to turn our faces north for Manson Creek, but this time, although we still had to walk the one hundred and twenty miles, we had no heavy packs on our backs. I had borrowed a .22 rifle and Bill a double-bitted axe. We were looking forward to the trip — it would be quite leisurely after our previous hike. Les was there to see us leave and shook hands with us, wishing us the best of luck. It was the last time we saw him, ever. He was killed in a light plane crash near Chilliwack about two years afterwards. I saw his picture and read the account of the accident in the newspaper. The news really saddened me, because he was a fine, healthy young man.

The trip back to Manson was, for the most part uneventful, but some things stand out with clarity and will be related as they occurred. The first was Bob Dunsmore's introduction to citronella oil. We carried this as a fly repellant, but Bob had never used it.

Crossing the first swampland about nine miles out of the Fort, the mosquitoes hit us in clouds. Bill and I promptly applied a little of the citronella oil to the forehead, ears, back of the neck, and hands, but Bob just scoffed at us using "that stinking stuff" as he called it. However, he found the leafy branch he was using as a switch was no match for the mosquitoes, so he asked to use the citronella. Before we could say anything to warn him, he had poured some in the palm of his hand and splashed it all over his forehead. Of course much ran into his eyes and he let out a yell which could be heard a mile away. Anyone who has used it knows, no matter how hard the lids of the eyes are closed, the citronella can seep its way between.

Bob was stamping around with eyes shut tight and yelling, "Wipe it off! Wipe it off! Get this damn stuff off me!" Finally we convinced him it would do no harm to his eyes and, after wiping away the excess, we told him to open his eyes just a little at a time. After he had calmed down and found he could still see as well as ever, he seemed a little sheepish about his panic. He admitted he really thought it might blind him. Instead, by using it judiciously, it really helped him. For years he had suffered an unexplained rash on his forehead, but by the time we reached Manson it had disappeared completely and never again did it return.

Late in the afternoon we came to the one remaining soft spot on the Juniper Straight section of the road. The driver, Earl, climbed down from the wagon and looked it over. It was bad and there was no alternative route around it. We had already waded it twice and knew what to expect. We should have unloaded most of the supplies and portaged them across. Earl decided to chance it because it would have taken too much time to portage.

59

The horses made a valiant effort and had almost reached firm ground on the other side, when one of the big grey "wheelers" went down and stayed down. Earl quickly calmed the lead horses because they were panicky and trying to reach the firm ground just ahead. Bill and I moved as fast as possible in the muck to help the big grey. It was lying there inert, its head almost entirely buried. I grasped an ear and Bill the halter strap and we both gave a mighty heave. Its head came out of the mud and we could hear a great "whoosh" of air enter the nostrils and lungs. The poor thing just lay there, its sides heaving, and after a few minutes showed signs of recovery.

Fortunately the other grey "wheeler" had not attempted to move, but stood belly deep in the mud. Earl then unhitched the remaining horses and took them to the firm ground, where his wife kept them under control. The mired grey could not stand up, even when unhitched, so deeply were its legs embedded, so Earl hooked onto it with the other grey and finally managed to pull it to its feet and bring it to firm ground. It was shaking in every limb with the effort, so we decided not to try to proceed further that day.

We packed much of the heavy load from the wagon to dry ground and prepared to camp for the night. Earl fed the horses, but tethered them with their harness on because he wanted to pull out the almost empty wagon after we had all eaten a meal. There was lots of good stout rope for this, although he had not expected to use it until the steep grades on Baldy Mountain were reached. Tying one end of a double rope on the wagon tongue and hooking the four bay "cayuses" on the other, the lightened wagon came out of the mud without too much effort. After that he unharnessed and turned the team loose to forage. There were patches of good feed beside the road. However, he kept his big saddle horse tethered because he used it every morning to round up the other six horses.

Earl not only dressed like a cowboy, he really was one of the best. He could rope and ride, and had ridden in many stampedes against other top-notch performers. His wife, too, was first class. They were training their little girl to follow their footsteps. She was absolutely fearless, riding the stallion Earl used as a saddle horse. I think we were all glad to relax for the night.

Around five the next morning Earl rode out to round up the team. They were not too far away, and he had no trouble herding them back to the wagon. The grey which had been mired seemed all right, but once we got rolling again, it was plain to see it was not. It obviously could not pull hard. Earl was extremely gentle with horses and did not force it, so we slowed down considerably. We were five days reaching the Nation River, where we camped on the edge of a small meadow.

Bill went to cut down a dry tree for firewood, when the axe glanced off the side and struck his boot. He put a gash in his big toe alongside the nail. Fortunately it struck neither bone nor tendon. Neither of us knew anything about first aid, and the only antiseptic was a bottle of creolin which Bill had. He poured in some of this, tore up a handkerchief, and bandaged it. This was a mistake, as Bill quickly found out. The creolin should have been diluted, but as it was not, it burned all the surface tissue on his big toe. It caused him much suffering for several days, and the "cure" was much worse than the wound from the axe. On top of his misery, the cut boot allowed water and dirt to enter.

The weather had been favourable since leaving the Fort, but a sudden change on the sixth day out brought cold northerly winds and heavy rain squalls. We made slow progress and evening found us about nine miles beyond our starting point of the morning. Bill's foot bothered him. In addition, the grade from the Nation River was quite steep in several places for the first four or five miles. The horses were very tired, so Earl decided to make camp early, because the toughest part was yet to come.

We were all pleasantly surprised to find Skookum Davidson already camped in the meadow where we had decided to stay for the night. He was on his way to the mine at Slate Creek with an extremely large spool of cable. This was a wagon load in itself. Skook had little else on the wagon except his grub, bedroll, snatch-blocks, and coils of heavy rope. Four horses comprised his team. There was a large fire already blazing and the sight made me feel much better, because my legs were wet and cold. Bill, Bob, and I began supper as soon as we could, even before fixing up for the night. Earl's wife and Skook were on the opposite side of the fire preparing theirs.

Skook had a large frying pan full of morels he had found among the pines. I am very fond of the common meadow mushroom and had no trouble identifying them, even as a child — but this panful of Skook's was the most villainous, poisonous looking mess I had ever seen! However, they smelled delicious as they cooked, and Skook ate them with very obvious enjoyment. I was curious as to their name, but he knew them only as morels. Because there were many species of that name, it did not explain much. The following day we found more. Despite their repulsive appearance, they were excellent fried in butter with a sprinkle of salt and pepper added.

It was much better having another team for company, as Skook travelled ahead of Earl. The wind had moderated somewhat, but was still raw and cold. By evening we had arrived at Gillis' Grave where large meadows provided ample feed for the horses. Bob Dunsmore had a small box camera along, and I snapped his picture by the side of the grave.

The evening of the next day found us camped on the lower slopes of Baldy Mountain. Despite the fact that it was now midsummer, we were glad of the comforting warmth of a large campfire, the wind being very chilly. It was here, after supper, that Skook regaled us with stories of the terrible creatures which roamed the slopes of Baldy. Even the mighty grizzly gave these fearsome brutes a wide berth, for according to Skook, they were impervious to bullets. Larger than a bear, they had a very peculiar build. Their mouths were shaped like old-fashioned can openers. In addition, they had two short legs on one side of the body and two long legs on the other, which made them perfectly at home on the steep sidehills.

He solemnly advised us to carry at least two unopened cans of milk in our pockets at all times while on Baldy. It was one of two means a person had of outwitting these beasts, should one pick up a man's trail. The thing to do was to throw a can of milk at the brute when it was too close for comfort, whereupon it would stop to open it with its can opener mouth. This gave the intended victim a chance to look for a large, flat area, and, on finding one, the person had to stand perfectly still in the centre of it. Of course the "sidehill gouger," as this beast was called, could only run in circles on a flat surface, owing to the short legs on one side of the body. As long as the victim did not move, he was perfectly safe. All he had to do was to wait until the beast had completely exhausted itself running in circles around him. When it had collapsed, he was free to walk away. We solemnly assured Skook we would carry some canned milk in our pockets until we had crossed Baldy. With this and many other stories he kept us entertained until it was time to turn in, and so passed a very pleasant evening on the mountain slopes.

Breaking camp early the next day, it was not long before we encountered the first of the excessively steep grades on the road over the mountain. The horses were unhitched from the loaded wagons and were driven up the slopes, with the wagon doubletrees still hooked to the traces. After climbing a hundred feet or so, they were turned around facing downhill. A long rope was then tied to the wagon tongue and the free end was brought up the hill, passed through a snatch-block which had been anchored to the base of a convenient balsam tree, then fastened to the doubletrees which were still attached to the traces. Earl, Bob, Bill, and I then obtained good stout poles each about six feet in length and took stations alongside each wagon wheel. These poles were to jam in the wheel spokes, should the rope break when the wagon was being towed up the steep slope. On Skook's command the horses took up the strain on the rope, then proceeded at a steady pace down the road, and so passed the wagon as it was towed uphill. Once the wagon had almost reached the snatch-block, the horses held it there until we had blocked the wheels safely.

Thus all the steep grades uphill were overcome in a like manner. It was a slow process, but the best one possible under the circumstances. By late afternoon we had reached the flat plateau over the summit. We camped to make lunch for overselves and feed the horses, because many hours had passed. I particularly remember the meal — Bill and I were so ravenous we ate the first batch of pancakes half raw!

Many of the depressions of the summit still had plenty of snow in them, but the road kept to the higher ridges and was bare. There was no danger of sliding off into a ravine, as the cat had done on our previous trip out from Manson.

After a good meal and rest we hitched up the teams again and pushed on, because there was still plenty of daylight left at that altitude. It was almost sundown when we stopped to camp for the night. We were about halfway down the opposite slope. To brake the wagons on the steep grades downhill we put rough-locks on the wheels, and twice we had to lock all four wheels for short distances. It was almost noon the next day before we were moving again. The big grey horse which had been mired was getting weaker each day, and Earl fed it some oats and let it have a good rest.

Skook had pushed on ahead. He was taking the fork in the road which went to the C. M. & S. mine on Slate Creek, while we were going directly to the Manson Creek placer diggings.

As we slowly descended the mountain the air got much warmer. On reaching the foot of Baldy, we unhooked the horses and let them forage. We made camp early on the banks of Manson Creek.

Bill and Bob said they would prepare camp and make supper, so I took a walk along the road we would be travelling the next day. I had the .22 rifle with me and it was not long before I shot a rabbit. When I returned to camp I gave it to Bill, who soon dressed it. Bob cut it up and fried it. He was preparing the supper, so we had fried rabbit to help out the evening meal.

We had planned on an early start for the next day, hoping to reach Kildare Gulch before noon, but things did not work out to schedule. Earl had quickly rounded up the foraging horses except the sick grey. It was not with the others, so he made a second trip to find it while we were finishing breakfast. We were all packed and the other horses harnessed, when he returned without it. He told us he had found it, but it had died sometime during the night. It was lying in a willow thicket about half a mile away from camp. I felt sorry to hear the news. The poor brute had never recovered from the mire on Juniper Straight.

However, the balance of the trip to Kildare Gulch was easily made by using four horses, and one was tethered behind the wagon. On our arrival the horses were unhitched, but not turned loose. The cayuses had now to serve as pack horses to deliver the supplies to various miners scattered along Manson Creek. Bill, Bob, and I were going to take a short cut from Kildare Gulch to Lost Creek, but before leaving we had a bite to eat.

It was now that Earl received his first customer. He looked Chinese to me and had walked up the steep trail which led from the diggings at the bottom of the gulch. He offered Earl a glass bottle containing what appeared to me to be a small amount of gold. On a pasted label on the side of the bottle was printed the exact weight of the gold inside. The Chinaman wanted to trade it for potatoes, which Earl weighed on a crude handmade scale. Who got the better of the bargain I do not know, but it seemed like a lot of spuds for a little of the yellow metal. However, there was no denying we were now in the country where the stuff could be found, and we were here to get as much as we could before freeze-up.

Forfar's Hotel, Fort St. James, B.C.

From left to right: Ed Forfar, Bill Faith, Hans Madsen, Gerry Affie, Oscar Nygaard and Bill Kinniburgh at Forfar's Hotel.

Fire of 1938 near Manson Creek Settlement.

McCorkell Flume crossing Slate Creek near its confluence with Manson Creek, 1933.

The C. M. & S. Mine on Slate Creek, 1936.

Slate Creek Settlement before mining operations commenced, 1934.

Skookum Davidson and his pack horses crossing the Nation River
Bridge.

Positioning the boiler for the C. M. & S. Mine on Slate Creek.

Exhausted horses breaking trail on Baldy Mountain.

Bob Dunsmore at Gillis' grave, Old Baldy Road, 1935.

Captain Bob Adams, centre; Jack Adams on his left.

Bill Faith's cat train preparing to ascend Baldy Mountain.

Bill Faith at front of his cat train transporting a load of pipe for the Germansen Mine.

A spot of trouble on the Baldy Mountain Road!

Going . . . going . . . Slate Creek operations.

Freighting on the Manson Creek Road after *improvements* to the Juniper Straight Section, 1938.

Lost Creek

It was with light hearts that Bill and I now shouldered our packs, which contained only blankets and personal effects, for the three-mile hike to our journey's end, "Lost Creek." Earl was to bring our grub supplies the following day, using the pack horses.

We descended the extremely steep trail to the bottom of the gulch and here saw the first evidence of the work done by the miners of the 1870's. Row after row of "tailings" — hand-piled rocks and boulders too large to pass through the sluice boxes used by the old-timers. Many remains of old buildings were still visible, and it is thought that as many as twenty-five hundred miners were working in the Kildare Gulch area during the height of the gold fever.

Bob Dunsmore had a little trouble picking up the trail through the maze of tailings, but once we located it, the walking was good to Lost Creek. Here we met his son Jim, and once the introductions were over, he showed us to a small cabin to be used for sleeping. There were two rough wooden bunks inside. After fixing up the bunks with spruce boughs, we went back to the larger cabin, which also served as a cookhouse.

Jim Dunsmore was a dark-haired fellow of medium build and height. I guessed his age to be around thirty because he was very agile in his movements. It surprised me to learn he was forty-three. He was also a very smooth talker and completely fooled Bill and me for a considerable period of time.

We dined that night on rice and raisins, because that was the only food in the cabin, until our supplies came the next day. After supper we discussed plans to commence mining on our own, but Jim gradually talked us out of that idea. He suggested we pool our grub and come in with him on a tunnelling project, and his father, Bob Dunsmore, could act as cook. He assured us it was only a matter of a couple of week's work to tunnel through rimrock into a fantastically rich channel which had been buried by glaciers during the last Ice Age. He promised us twenty-five per cent of all gold found.

73

Strangely enough, there was some truth in the story. We saw the evidence next day that at least two tunnels had tapped the channel. The first one was alleged to have been driven by a man named MacKinnon in the first gold rush, and the second was driven by none other than Billy Steele, whom we had already met. These tunnels had been driven from the downstream side, but Jim's idea was to take a shortcut by cutting through the rim to gain entry to the bottom of the channel. It sounded feasible enough, in fact almost too simple. Why had not someone thought of it before?

Under Jim's guidance Bill and I set to work with enthusiastic energy, because he was an excellent miner with experience in all phases of mining. It was slow, laborious work, and the only way we could penetrate the rim was to bore holes, using drill steel and sledge-hammer, then load the holes with blasting powder. After the blasting operation we would "muck-out" into a mining car, then repeat the process. Jim showed us how to "bar-down" after blasting, to make sure there was no loose rock hanging in the roof of the tunnel.

Seven days a week for two weeks we toiled away at the rock face, which we had penetrated to a length of some thirty feet without showing any sign of breaking through to the channel. Toward the end of the third week, Bill, who was "single-jacking" a hole in the top corner of the tunnel, let out a yell as his drill suddenly broke through the rock wall into gravel. We were tremendously excited, and even Bob Dunsmore came up to look.

It did not take long to load the hole and light the fuse, after which we hurried out of the tunnel to await the explosion. Outside, we laughed and joked because we were all confident we were on the brink of making a big strike. The explosion came loud and sharp, not like the dull, heavy thud to which we had grown accustomed. "Bootleg!" said Jim. Sure enough, the powder charge had wasted its energy on a backward force in the gravel.

However, it had enlarged the drill hole to about a foot in diameter, and there was no mistaking we had indeed broken through to the channel. It did not take us long to remove the remaining slab of rim-rock, and by evening we had a complete gravel face to work on. We had so eagerly looked forward to this day. Now it had arrived we felt disappointed and let down because, despite repeated panning, the gravel had failed to yield a single "colour" of gold.

Jim assured us we had struck the channel too high on the rim, and that all we had to do was to sink a shaft inside the tunnel until we hit bedrock. Again it sounded simple, but Bill and I were doing all the work, and Jim the supervising. Most of the day he lay on his bunk dreaming of what he intended to do with his millions.

After supper Bill and I decided we would walk over to Slate Creek to see our friend Billy Steele. We intended to find out if we were wasting our time on this work, because Billy knew all about the channel. We also wanted to find out if the report of the amount of gold recovered by him was true, and if it was, why had he not continued to work the channel. Billy surprised us after the usual greeting by saying he expected to see us, because he had heard some time ago that we were back in Manson Creek country.

In a short time we brought the conversation around to the Lost Creek channel and asked if it were true he had really found much gold there. He said it was quite true, the channel was rich in spots. The pay streak was very good on the bedrock, but veered from one rim to the other. He said one car of a half yard of paydirt contained more than ninety ounces of gold, but most averaged around six ounces to the yard up to a foot in depth above bedrock. Above this the pay was poorer until five or six feet from bedrock where there was none at all.

We then asked the second part of our question. Why, if the pay was good, had he not continued working the channel? The answer was simple, "Bad air!" This had never occurred to us. Billy then went on to describe how he had put down a ninety foot air shaft so he could continue as far as he had. To proceed further meant sinking another shaft down to his tunnel again, so he gave up the idea. In any case, he made quite a few thousand dollars, which would last for years in that country.

We found his information not only helpful, but stimulating. We now knew for sure there was gold to be found on bedrock — if we could only get there. The problem of bad air could easily be licked in these days, with a small air compressor on the surface to force air through underground piping for hundreds of feet.

Before we left, Billy warned us to be careful of Jim, and said we should draw up a contract showing we were to receive a quarter of the gross amount of gold recovered — if and when we produced any.

The following day we commenced tunnelling in the gravel. We now had to use timber posts to support the roof. Again, Jim showed us how to set them up and how to make and drive "lagging" between each set of timbers. It was compressed gravel and easy to hold and we could drive six feet between sets. Soon it was time to start sinking the shaft in the tunnel in the hope of getting down to bedrock. The going was very slow because all the gravel had to be hoisted and dumped in the mine car. This, in turn, had to be trammed outside, and then the gravel put through a sluice box, which had been set up, because we knew if there was any gold in it we would be getting close to bedrock.

Days passed, and still no gold. By now two more problems faced us. The air in the bottom of the shaft was getting progressively worse the deeper we went. Water was beginning to seep into the shaft. Each morning we had to bail more and more, because it always filled to the same level.

Finally the day came when our candles would barely give a glimmer of light at the bottom of the shaft due to lack of oxygen. In addition, the water was coming in almost as fast as we could bail it. As we had neither water pumps, nor a compressor, we had to abandon the project. It was a bitter, hard blow to take, especially after the weeks of toil and the knowledge that the gold was somewhere beneath our feet.

The summer was quickly passing, and so far we had not produced even a colour of gold. Jim now came up with the idea we should try to sink another shaft alongside the present Lost Creek. To overcome the water problem he would build a water wheel to drive a "Chinese pump." To do this a dam and flume had to be built to give the desired pressure to drive the water wheel, which in turn was to supply the power to operate the pump.

Again Bill and I supplied the brawn, as Jim initiated us in the art of whip-sawing approximately one thousand board feet of lumber from a stand of spruce timber almost three miles from our camp on Lost Creek. We backpacked every inch of it by lashing three boards on each side of our pack-boards. With Bill bringing up the rear because he was an inch or two taller than I, we were able to travel the rocky, narrow trail up the Lost Creek Canyon.

It was exhausting work, but eventually the lumber was all transported for Jim to construct the flume and water wheel, while we were making the dam across Lost Creek. At last, all was in readiness and the water was turned into the flume. As the pressure built up behind the paddles of the big wheel, it slowly began to revolve. So far, everything was a success, so Bill and I began the task of shaft sinking.

Jim was constructing his "Chinese pump." We were down about six feet in the shaft when the water was too much to continue bailing, so Jim set up his pump. It consisted of a number of five-pound lard pails hooked on an endless belt, the lower end of which was down in the shaft. Another belt running from the water wheel turned the contraption, and each pail filled with water from the shaft emptied into a trough as it reached and passed over the top pulley. It worked well for a time, but eventually we had to add more pails as the shaft got deeper, to take care of the added influx of water. Finally the water wheel could not generate enough power to overcome the added weight of the water pails, and so ended another effort to mine the bedrock of Lost Creek.

Desperately, we tried another idea of Jim's — an automatic boom-gate. This too, worked, but the force of the backed up water was insufficient when released to tear down the banks of the creek downstream, as we had hoped. Fall was rapidly approaching, our grub supplies were dangerously low, yet we had not made a nickel.

I had not been feeling very well for some little time, as every day I had a headache. My face was badly swollen and I hardly recognized myself when I looked in a mirror. Suddenly, one night a terrible pain hit me in the back and side. It was impossible to lie quietly in bed, and I crawled up and down on my hands and knees on the trail outside the cabin. I could not keep back the groans of agony. Finally, Bill aroused Jim and Bob Dunsmore in the cookhouse.

It was warm in there. Jim offered me his bed and he used mine in our cabin. Despite the warmth, I could not lie still because the agony was so severe. After a time, I jumped out of bed and just made it to the door, where I started to vomit. I was fairly sure by now that I was suffering from a kidney stone, because somewhere I had read of the acute pain it could cause. After the bout of vomiting, the pain began to diminish somewhat, and I crawled back into bed. Gradually, I passed into an exhausted sleep, although I realized it was now daylight.

I stayed in bed for three days and ate nothing. Two miners from a few miles away came to see me and brought some Sal Hepatica, which seemed to do me some good. The facial swelling disappeared and I began to feel more normal.

As I recovered in strength, Bill and I began to think of returning home for the winter, because it was now the end of September. There was only about enough grub left to get us back to the Fort, because most of our supplies had been pooled with Dunsmores', who brought in much less than we.

Jim still wanted us to stay for another couple of weeks, to try another drift further downstream. He told us he was going to raise some money somehow during the winter so we could return the next year, with pumps and compressor, to complete the channel project we had been forced to abandon. We did not know whether to believe this story or not.

We were naturally disappointed that all our efforts had failed to produce any gold, not only for ourselves, but for Bob's sake as well. We had found him to be a fine old fellow. The day soon came when we said goodbye, because we heard the freighter was in Manson and would be leaving for Fort St. James. We left most of the supplies for Jim and his Dad to carry on for at least a couple more weeks.

Some Work in Chilco

All Bill and I had in the way of food was several pounds of rolled oats, a little tea and sugar, a small can of peanut butter, and some bannock which Bob had baked for us. I carried the .22 rifle and Bill the axe. We hoped to shoot some small game on the way out. Earl, the freighter, told us we could put our packs on the wagon, but we would have to walk.

The trip back to the Fort was made without any trouble. Near Gillis' Grave we picked up the supplies of a government surveyor, his helper, and his cook, and transported them on the wagon for several miles, where the camp was again set up. It was cold and wet, so we helped them set up the tents and stoves and put all their supplies under cover.

The engineer (whose name, I believe, was Guire) invited us to eat supper with them and stay overnight. George Ellis, the cook, put up an excellent supper, which seemed all the more appetizing under warm, dry conditions, because by this time it was raining heavily outside. At this point I should mention the surveyor's helper whose name was Jack Roberts. Our paths crossed again several years later in the Manson area.

We left early the next morning on another lap. The weather was still cold, but at least the rain had let up for the time being. A day's journey from the Fort, we camped at a creek called Thirty-One Mile. Earl and his wife bedded down under the wagon, while Bill and I "doubled up" for warmth in the open. Around two a.m. hailstones pelting on our faces woke us. We pulled the top canvas cover over our heads and promptly went back to sleep, because we were quite warm. It was with surprise we awoke around seven a.m. to find at least three inches of snow had fallen. Earl had a good campfire going. Apart from the hail rousing us, we had slept like a couple of hibernating bears.

However, the snowstorm seemed to have cleared the weather. It was sunny and warm again on our last day's trek into Fort St. James. We slept that night in the familiar camping ground.

"Well, here we were, back again!" We took stock of ourselves the following morning. A summer's work for nothing, grubstake gone, and flat broke! All the grub we had was a pound or so of mush and a fool-hen I had shot — not even a little salt for flavour. Things did not look favourable, especially with winter not far off.

We ate the last of the mush for breakfast, and Bill was cleaning the fool-hen, which we figured to have at the noon meal, if a small bird could be classed as a meal for two hungry men. A man of slim build approached us. He introduced himself as Buster Huffman and said he had a place at Souchie Creek. He asked us if we were interested in working for him a couple of days, digging spuds? He said the wages would only be a dollar fifty a day, but he would give us board.

It sounded real good to us, so we packed up and put our gear on his cabin boat. The crossing took longer than Bill and I had thought because Stuart Lake was wide at this point. After lunch at his home, we commenced digging potatoes. The work was very easy for us, and at the end of one and a half days the potatoes were dug, dried, and sacked. The weather continued ideal, so Buster found us other jobs to complete around his place. After three days he paid us four dollars and fifty cents each and took us back to Fort St. James.

Having a few dollars in our pockets made us feel better. We caught a ride to Vanderhoof on a freight truck. On arrival, the driver asked us to pay him two dollars each. He said his boss had told him to charge that amount. We did not believe him and said so — very emphatically. We proffered one dollar each, which he put in his own pocket without any hesitation. We were willing to bet his boss never saw any part of it.

We then went over to Chuey's restaurant for a slice of pie and coffee. Chuey was behind the counter as we walked in. He beamed. "Hallo, boys! You back again from Manson? How much gold you get?" We sat on the counter stools and said we had none, despite all the hard work we had done. He listened intently as we outlined our experiences, trying to chase down the yellow metal. "Oh, well!" he commented, "You young fellows maybe lucky more, next year. You go back, eh?" Concern crossed the broad Oriental face. "You boys hungry?" When we said we had some money he replied, "Well, this pie and coffee yours, anyway." He left to serve another customer.

Soon he was back and said, "Why you not try road boss for job?" He then went on to explain that there had been some government work on the roads for a time, because something had to be done to try and alleviate the acute conditions. People were desperate. We knew that and we were single. How much worse it was for the married with families to support.

Bill and I left our packs in the restaurant and walked over to the office of Bob Reid, the road superintendent. Bob listened to what we had to say about our trip north and our request for some road work. As we concluded, he replied, "Yes, I'll give you ten days work on a slashing job near Finmore. You boys have at least tried to find something. There's a lot around this town who won't make any effort at all." That probably was not quite fair, because there were no jobs — but we were elated at the news of ten days work each at two dollars and eighty cents a day.

Bob then gave us a sealed envelope to hand to a Mr. Finlayson at Finmore, who would show us where to commence work. He told us also we should take our own food, because there was no cookhouse, only tents for sleeping.

We slept at our homes in Chilco that night. It was not easy to return empty-handed after being away for months, but our folks were glad to see us. We were certainly glad to see them. Dad was particularly interested in hearing about the Manson Creek country, because he was the type who found any story of adventure fascinating.

The following day we reported to Mr. Finlayson to commence work. He showed us what he wanted done, then left us, because he was suffering severely from a stomach ulcer. By now the nights were quite cold, and we had to keep up the fire in the tent heater. The ten days passed quickly, and we walked to Vanderhoof to report we were finished. Bob Reid told us we each would receive a cheque for twenty-eight dollars in a few days time.

We then called on George Ogston and each of us managed to get a contract to hew two hundred and fifty ties. Altogether, things did not look too bad. After all, we would have a little money, plus the money the ties would bring us during the winter months.

Christmas of 1935 and the New Year of 1936 found us in good health and spirits. Times were still desperately hard, but everyone seemed to keep well in the little communities. Pleasures were simple and, looking back over the years, all the more enjoyable for that reason.

Big game was plentiful and was always shared with the neighbours. The bush was full of rabbits, willow grouse, and spruce hen. Each family would have a little card game, either whist or cribbage, on Saturday night. Quite often several families would get together and hold these games, competing for home-made prizes, with a special "booby" prize for the unlucky person with the lowest score. It was good, wholesome fun, with none of the drinking, bitterness, and jealousies so prevalent in the later, more affluent times.

Nineteen Thirty-Six

Towards the end of March in 1936, Bill and I received a letter from our friend, Bob Dunsmore, who had spent the winter in Prince George. It contained very good news. A private company had been formed in Edmonton to raise capital to mine the channel on Lost Creek! The company was capitalized at twenty thousand dollars, of which several thousand had already been raised, and forwarded to them in Prince George to buy the necessary equipment.

The letter went on to invite us to spend a holiday with Bob and his wife in Prince George during April. All we had to do was to tell them the date when we could join them, and they would send us the tickets for the train journey.

This was wonderful news indeed! Now we were assured of a job all summer on a payroll, plus the percentage promised us, should we strike paydirt. It was almost incredible! Yet the letter was there to prove it was not imagination. Naturally, Bill and I were very elated and excited about the sudden turn in our fortunes, and even our folks caught some of the enthusiasm. It took but a few minutes to write a letter in reply, saying we could be in Prince George any time it was convenient for Bob and his wife.

In a few days we received another letter from Bob, containing the money for our train fares, plus a dollar each extra for meals. On our arrival in Prince George, Bob was at the station to meet us. We walked to his home, which was only a few blocks from the depot, where Mrs. Dunsmore greeted us warmly.

She showed us to our room. After a wash and general clean-up, we joined them in the livingroom. Over tea and cake, the conversation naturally got around to mining and what we hoped to accomplish during the coming summer. Suddenly Bill asked, "Where's Jim?" Bob's face changed as he paused before answering, "Oh, he's around town somewhere." Then, fiercely, "He's playing the big shot — spending money like a drunken sailor! And it's not his money, either!" he added. It was obvious Bob and his wife disapproved of the way their son was acting. But, because he had been appointed

83

manager by the Edmonton company, there was nothing they could do about it.

It was several days later when Jim showed up at his parents' home. He extended us a lukewarm greeting — almost disdainfully. What a change from the man who had been glad to share our grub in Manson! He was dressed in the latest fashion. However, once he commenced talking mining, he was more like the fellow we had known. He certainly had grandiose plans and was positive the mine would produce lots of gold. Well, it would have to produce, to realize all the things Jim had in mind. Even twenty-thousand dollars would only accomplish a fraction of his proposals. After supper Jim left us to return to his room at one of the hotels downtown. Yes, he was certainly living it up on his new-found wealth.

We stayed with the Dunsmores until the last week in April. During that time, we saw Jim twice. On the last occasion he told us we would be flying in to Manson from Fort St. James just as soon as the lake was free of ice. We were making progress! From foot-slogging with heavy packs on our backs to flying. Nineteen hundred and thirty-six was, indeed a momentous year, not only for us, but for the whole of Vanderhoof and other district communities.

On our return to Chilco, our folks were naturally pleased to hear how much we had enjoyed our visit with the Dunsmores and the fact we had the promise of well-paid employment all the coming summer months. Jim had told us before leaving Prince George, that the day we boarded the plane at Fort St. James, we would be on the company payroll at fifty cents an hour, plus free board. It was hard to realize our good fortune — that was a tremendous wage in those days.

Bill and I spent the few remaining days around our homes, preparing for the "great adventure." This time I was taking two rifles, a 6.5 Mannlicher carbine for big game and my .22, seeing that I did not have to carry them. We each managed to buy a new pair of rubber boots, plus shirts, socks, etc.

At last came the great day we received word from Bob to journey to Fort St. James and that he and Jim would join us. On arrival at the Fort, we found the Dunsmores already there. They had rented a small cabin on Huffman's Point, and there were a couple of spare cots for Bill and me. The plane from Edmonton was due in any day, because the lake was free of the winter's ice. The weather was quite warm because it was now almost the middle of May.

In addition to several hundred pounds of food, the Dunsmores had brought in two portable centrifugal pumps, five ten-gallon drums of gasoline, and a carton of motor oil. Also there was blasting powder and a number of new picks, shovels, drill steel, etc., as well as numerous other small items. It was obvious the plane would have to make more than one trip to transport men and material to Manson.

Fort St. James was again seeing an influx of transients, all intent on one thing — to make the trip into Manson Creek as soon as road conditions permitted. A year ago we were among this crowd of transients, full of hope and impatient to get going. Now we were awaiting a plane to fly us there, with all expenses paid. Truly, the wheel of fortune had turned in our direction, and many of the boys told us how lucky we were. No one knew that better than we.

On the evening of the third day after our arrival, the plane arrived from Edmonton. There was quite a flurry of excitement. Aircraft were not too common, and this one was the first float-plane of the season. Many local people and transients gathered at Huffman's Point to watch it tie up. The pilot had no lack of willing hands to help.

He was a tall, good-looking fellow and carried himself with an air which seemed exclusive to the bush pilot. Let there be no mistake, these pilots were good flyers, self-reliant and courageous. They had to be to survive. Thus it was, that sultry May evening, we met Ernie Kubichek, pilot of a United Air Transport plane from Edmonton. (It would seem appropriate to mention that this plane was owned by Grant MacConachie, who later became president of Canadian Pacific Airlines, the second largest airline in Canada.) Ernie Kubichek flew for Grant and Canadian Pacific for many years. Sad to relate, he met his death not at the controls of some rickety bush plane, but in the captain's seat of an airliner on the Prince George-Vancouver run. Despite the later up-to-date navigational aids, the aircraft, for some forever unknown reason, failed to clear the summit of Mt. Cheam and all aboard perished.

Early next morning we were due to take off for Manson, where we were to land on one of the string of lakes a few miles from the mining area. Stuart Lake was glassy calm and the pilot could not get the high-wing monoplane to lift off. Bob Dunsmore and Bill were aboard with half the supplies. Jim and I were going on the second trip with the balance. After several abortive attempts to lift

off, Ernie taxied back and said we had better wait awhile for a wind
to help. If one did not start to blow by ten o'clock, then he would try
again, after pumping out some fuel from the tanks. Luck was with
us. By ten a.m. a brisk west wind was blowing down the lake, and
the float-plane had no difficulty heading into it and taking off.

Jim made a trip to one of the stores during the plane's absence.
He returned accompanied by a slim, blonde fellow of about my age.
He introduced him as Ernie Floyd and said that he was an experienced miner, who would be working with us in Manson Creek. I
took an instinctive liking to him, and this friendship was to last us
the rest of our lifetimes. However, this in no way affected my partnership with Bill.

We had started to eat lunch when the plane landed after the
return from Manson. The pilot said that no difficulty had been
experienced on landing on one of the Manson Lakes. They, too,
were free of ice. We soon had the plane loaded with more supplies
and gear. After refueling, Jim, Ernie Floyd, and I climbed into the
cabin and found ourselves seats wherever we could. The lake was
quite choppy, due to the brisk wind, and before the plane became
completely airborne, the pontoons were hitting every wave with a
bone-jarring wallop. However, once airborne, the lake quickly
dropped away, and we got a close-up view of the side of Mt. Pope.

The trip was a little bumpy in places, but otherwise uneventful. I
truthfully enjoyed every minute of it. All too soon, the pilot cut the
motor as we approached the Manson Lakes for a landing. We unloaded the supplies and put them with the balance of the first load.
Bill and Bob Dunsmore had walked on to Lost Creek, taking only
their bedrolls.

Jim asked me to stay with the supplies, because the plane was
going to make a third trip before nightfall. He and Ernie Floyd
would walk on to Lost Creek, and I would stay behind, help the
pilot unload the supplies after the third trip, and camp there overnight to guard the grub against any possible marauding animals.
Because I was the only one who owned a high-powered rifle, I was
naturally chosen. Jim said he would get some pack horses the next
day, and he would have the supplies brought to the camp on Lost
Creek.

After the plane's third trip, and with all the grub under canvas,
I made my bed for the night. With a cheerful campfire blazing and a
good feed under my belt, I leaned back against a pine tree and

relaxed. It was good to be alive! I shall always remember that night. Not because of the things that happened, but — on the contrary — because of the solitude and magnificence of God's handiwork. Only when a person is alone and at peace does he really take time to appreciate his environment.

How long I stayed gazing at the magnificence of the heavens I did not attempt to estimate. Certainly it was quite dark, and the fire just a few embers before I stirred myself. How does a person describe a sunset he cannot actually see — only the rays which colour the peaks of the massive Wolverine Range, while the valley below is in darkness? It is beyond my limited efforts, but I know what I saw. I give thanks to my Creator that I was alive to see it and appreciate it.

After making up the fire I decided to seek my bed for awhile. I did not sleep, but gazed into the blackness of the bush beyond the range of the firelight. My thoughts went back over the events of the preceding year. Could this really be me, who was now on a payroll with prospects of making a fortune? Did I really fly into Manson today? Without intending to, I dozed for some time, and again when I awoke the fire was low.

"Heck!" I thought, "Here I am supposed to be guarding this grub, and I fall asleep. What a laugh that is — probably the most ferocious animal for miles around is a mouse. Oh, well, better not take any chances. There was always the odd chance that a wolverine might be in the vicinity," so ran my thoughts. I had never seen one of these creatures, but what I had heard of them was not good. It was said they would destroy or befoul anything they could not eat. They feared nothing, and even the mighty grizzly treated them with respect. Outside of trappers, very few people even knew what they looked like.

I got up and threw more wood on the fire. With my back toward it, I gazed out across the blackness of the lake. On the opposite side of the valley the black mass of the Wolverine Range was faintly discernible against a starlit sky. Wide awake now, I toasted myself in front of the fire until dawn. In the early light I made myself a pot of mush, then went back to bed. I figured it must be around three or four a.m. Might as well catch up on some sleep until the pack horses came to pick up the supplies.

It was late afternoon before I heard voices. Jim and Bill and an Indian fellow by the name of Za Basil had arrived with pack-boards to pick up some of the food for the camp in Lost Creek. Jim explained that the pack horses would not be in until the following day. He said I had better stay with the supplies for another night. I did not mind. The weather was good and I enjoyed being in the bush. Better still, I was getting paid for it. Again at sundown I watched the peaks of the Wolverine Mountains in the rays of the setting sun.

The pack horses came the next day, and the balance of the grub was loaded. Lashing my bedroll on my pack-board and with my rifle in the crook of my arm, I started ahead of them for Lost Creek, because the trail was easy to follow.

Some time later I was surprised to find a drilling crew at work on the Rossetti-Hayward property. This drill and crew had come overland from Takla, having started there the previous year. The man in charge was a Captain Bob Adams, and I believe was financially backed by the Hammill interests of Ontario. I was even more surprised to find Gus Sabo and Steve Firko, who had been with us part of the way on the tough trip over Baldy with Ogilvie, working on the drill. I spoke with them a few minutes, then continued on my way, after telling them I would visit them some evening when we had settled down at the Lost Creek camp.

On my arrival there I quickly made up my bed in the cabin Bill and I shared. It was quite comfortable and dry, and there was a cast-iron heater in case we needed some warmth.

The next day Jim laid out a plan to commence mining. The first job was cutting timbers and lagging for a new shaft. The way Jim had it figured was to abandon completely the previous year's work, and dig a new shaft. According to his estimate, if we sank a shaft alongside the present creek level to a depth of twenty feet below it, we could tunnel from the bottom of the shaft through the rimrock and strike the bottom of the old channel. Of course, it would be wet work all the way, but this time we had gas pumps to take care of the water.

The Hudson's Bay Company built and opened a store at the old Manson townsite in 1936. The first manager was a young fellow by the name of Jack Copeland, and his store was a great asset. It did much to bring in many men who might never have ventured into Manson. They were secure in the knowledge that at least they could purchase enough food to return to Fort St. James, should they not find any gold.

However, to get back to our own search for buried wealth, we were also secure in the knowledge that once we got to the bottom of the channel, we would find gold. Ernie Floyd, Bill, and I set to work with a will. Jim, of course, was manager and supervisor. Ernie, already an experienced miner, was to be in charge of the shaft sinking, and Bill his helper and mucker. Because of my knowledge of gasoline engines, I was to be pump-man. In my spare time I was to cut lagging and shape timbers. In addition, Jim elected me to be timekeeper and bookkeeper, which I could do in the evenings when off shift. Why he could not do this himself I never understood.

The shaft sinking proceeded slowly but surely. We had to use the primitive method of churn-drilling to bore holes in the rock. The holes were then loaded with sixty per cent blasting powder. With the fuses lit, Ernie and Bill would then scale the ladder to get out of the shaft and await the explosions. The muck would then be hoisted from the shaft by windlass, then a new round of holes bored, and the whole process repeated.

However, as we got deeper, we began to get many misfires owing to the amount of water collecting in the shaft, because naturally we had to cover the suction hose of the pump and hoist it sufficiently high to escape damage. Without the pump working, the water poured into the shaft and quickly covered the loaded holes. We tried using tar and soap on the fuses around the crimped caps, but we still got too many misfires.

We finally solved the problem by using liquid solder around the crimped ends of the caps. We would make up the fuses the night before, which allowed the liquid solder to harden into a watertight seal. With no more misfires, the shaft sinking proceeded at a faster rate, but it still was not fast enough to suit Jim. He started to talk of running two shifts. Because Bill, Ernie, and I were already working a twelve-hour shift, he would have to hire more men.

A few days later, when we entered the cookhouse at suppertime, Jim introduced us to a tall fellow named Einer Petersen, who would be starting to work with us as a miner. My partner Bill was to be his helper, and I would be Ernie Floyd's helper. We were now going to work two shifts of eight hours each, instead of one twelve-hour shift. This suited me fine, because now I would be able to get a little time off in the evenings, to do a little prospecting on my own.

We all liked "Pete," as everyone called him. He was a family man and lived with his wife and daughter in a cabin near Manson Creek.

He was washing out a little gold on a bench "digging" when Jim approached him about working on Lost Creek. Pete, a first class, hard-working man, had worked at the famous Hollinger mine in Ontario before moving west.

As we got deeper in the shaft, another problem arose, which had entirely been overlooked by everyone. This was the law which says a centrifugal pump can make a straight suction lift of thirty-two feet at sea level. As we were mining at more than three thousand feet above that level, our suction lift was much less than thirty-two feet. By the time we were down eighteen feet, we were having difficulty keeping it primed. If the least bit of air entered with the water, the prime was lost and the pump could not pick it up until it was again re-primed.

Another mistake was that the pumps should have been the self-priming type. We could not put the pumps in the shaft, either, due to the danger of the carbon monoxide fumes. Finally, by the time we were twenty-one feet deep, the pumps would lift no more.

Jim had altered his estimate of how deep the shaft should be to hit the bottom of the old channel. He now estimated at least twenty-six feet, although thirty feet would be better, if we could make it. There was nothing else to do but sink a smaller shaft of ten feet deep alongside the main shaft. In this we put the pump, then punched a small hole through the side wall into the main shaft. Through this hole we put a two-inch pipe, which was coupled to the suction inlet of the pump. On the other end we put the suction hose down the main shaft. Using this method, we were able to get down to thirty feet without danger from exhaust fumes.

It was slow, tedious, and expensive work. We had been paid regularly by cheque each month, but no one had cashed any. We did not need the money. Any small items we got from the Hudson's Bay we had charged, because our credit was good while we were employed.

I was doing a little panning downstream from the camp one evening, when two strangers came walking up the trail. One was thick-set with a heavy beard, the other much younger and clean shaven. The bearded man spoke as they stopped. "My name's Gilliam, Harry Gilliam." "I'm from Ontario," he added, "and this is Lee Scarfe from the prairies." I acknowledged the greeting and said I was working at the mine further upstream.

Gilliam again spoke, "Do you think there is a chance of getting a job with you? I'm a miner — I worked at the Hollinger back in

Ontario." The thought flashed through my mind, "What a coincidence! Pete is from the Hollinger, and now this fellow." Aloud I said, "You will have to ask the manager, as he does the hiring." I then proceeded to tell them where Jim could be found, so they walked on and I started to pan again.

I was lucky that evening, because I panned out all of a dollar in gold. One little nugget being worth at least two bits. I decided I would set up a sluice box in that spot the next evening.

On my way back to camp I called at Jim's cabin. Everyone was there except Bill and Pete, who were on shift. The two strangers had just finished eating, and the big fellow did most of the talking. Like many more they were jobless and broke. They had walked into Manson Creek, hoping to dig a little gold. It was a familiar story — had not Bill and I, along with others, had the same idea?

Jim could not give them employment right away, but said if they could get along for a week or so, he thought he might be able to hire them later. In the meantime he had to make a trip to Edmonton on business.

The big fellow appeared fascinated by the gold I had in my pan and seemed as if he had never seen any before. "How long did it take you to get it?" he asked. "Oh, about a couple of hours, I guess," I replied. "You must have at least five dollars there," he said. I laughed. "Oh, no, a dollar would be nearer the mark. The water appears to magnify the gold." "Just the same, I wish I could find a spot where I could pan like that," he said.

I felt sorry for them, because I knew only too well what it felt like in their present state. "Tell you what I'll do, if its okay with Jim," I replied. "I was going to set up a sluice box tomorrow evening, but instead I'll loan you my gold pan and you can pan there all day tomorrow." "Okay, Jim?" I asked, turning to him. "Fine with me," replied Jim, "Snipe all you want." "Snipe" is the common term for working by hand in shallow ground.

Jim wasn't a bad fellow at all, once he got away from the city. He fed the two fellows until they found enough gold to buy something at the Bay. He also let them have the little shack where Bill and I had first slept.

It was obvious from the start they knew nothing about placer work. They did not know the proper way to hold a gold pan. The following evening I set up a sluice box in the creek and showed them how it worked. They did not find much gold, but enough to buy plain food to live well enough and also a little tobacco.

I still spent my time prospecting after work and struck a nice little pocket of paydirt a few feet from the cabin Bill and I shared. In less than two hours, I washed out almost seventy dollars in gold. One nugget was worth nine dollars and sixty cents. Naturally we were all excited, but it proved to be just a little pocket which had been over-looked by the original discoverers of Lost Creek. Nevertheless, it showed how rich it must have been and gave an inkling what to expect when we got to the bottom of the old channel.

Soon after this Jim left for Edmonton. Before going he asked to buy what gold I had, because it would look better if he could show the shareholders some of the yellow metal. I hated to part with it, but could not very well refuse under the circumstances. However, I would not sell the biggest nugget. The cheque he gave me for the balance was cashed at the Bay, and Bill got half of it.

The shaft, by now, was down to thirty feet, and the tunnel commenced. We hoped to strike the bottom of the rich channel. We knew there would be forty or fifty feet of solid rock to tunnel through before this could happen. We were now travelling in a horizontal direction instead of vertical and had to commence single and double-jacking. This was done by striking the drill steel with a heavy hammer, and after each blow, the drill was turned slightly in the hole. It is a primitive method, but not as slow as some might imagine, especially in the slate-schist formations of Lost Creek.

We made fairly good time. Each day, as we got nearer, our excitement increased with the thought of the riches ahead. Then a new problem arose. Due to the fact that it was not easy to get rid of the smoke after blasting we began to get powder headaches.

By now Jim had returned from Edmonton. He seemed a little subdued, for some reason I could not fathom at the time.

It was in September when the day came which we knew had to come eventually. Someone's drill had to go through the solid rock into the channel, because by now we were running three shifts. Jim had hired Harry Gilliam and Lee Scarfe, and they soon acquired the mining know-how by watching us at work.

It was on Pete and Bill's shift that a hole was finally punched through the wall-rock into the channel. As the drill steel was withdrawn, water and fine gravel followed. The hole was loaded and the fuses lit. It was a tense, exciting minute. We waited on the surface for the explosion. We felt the thud and the tremor — then everything seemed to break loose down the shaft.

It was hard to see what had happened, due to the smoke, but we could hear the rush of water and the rumble of boulders. Quickly a pump was started, then the second. Only with both pumps running could the water level in the shaft be prevented from rising too rapidly. Despite this, the water, a rusty red in colour, gradually filled the tunnel and shaft to within twelve feet of the top.

Here we were, again fighting our old enemy, water. There was nothing else to do but continuously pump until we could drain the water from the old channel. Only after three full days of non-stop pumping was the water level in the shaft noticed to be dropping. A couple of days later, we exposed the muck and boulders in the bottom of the shaft. What a clean-up job was in front of us!

Everything had to be hoisted to the top by hand-windlass, and the bucket then dumped in a mine car. When the car was full of gravel we ran it over to the sluice boxes. The gravel, in turn, had to be washed through the sluices to trap any gold it might contain. It did contain a little gold, too. Enough to confirm that there would be gold ahead of us in the channel.

It was at this time I made a discovery which forced me to make one of the most difficult decisions I had ever been called upon to make. Another pay day was due, and as bookkeeper I was making up the time and writing out the pay cheques for Jim to sign. Among the recent mail was a bank statement showing there was slightly less than one thousand dollars to the company's credit. What a jolt that gave me!

Here was I, with around five hundred dollars in uncashed cheques, then Bill and Ernie with like amounts. Then came Pete, Harry Gilliam, and Lee Scarfe with smaller amounts. In addition there were other bills to pay. Where was the balance of the twenty thousand dollars which was supposed to have come from Edmonton.

I hardly slept that night! What should I do? Should I quit the job and cash my cheques while the bank would still honour them, or should I stick with the job when success seemed so imminent? I had been broke for so many years that five hundred dollars was a fortune to me. It would even take me for a trip back to the Old Country.

On the other hand, what about the percentage Jim had promised Bill and me when we struck the paydirt on the bottom of the channel? Maybe I would lose thousands of dollars if I left the job now. After months of effort I was just as anxious as anyone to see the bottom of that channel. What a dilemma! What a choice! With my brain trying to find the right answer, I fell into an uneasy sleep.

Came the morning, my mind was made up. I was leaving! But first I had to see Bill. He was my partner and had a right to know. He was still on shift, so I walked over to the shaft and called down for him to come up. I explained the situation and told him of my decision.

I could see the news was a shock to him and could see from the expression on his face that his brain was weighing up the pros and cons of the startling facts. Slowly he spoke, "I'll take a chance on bedrock." That decision cost him dearly, and as it turned out, maybe his life.

We shook hands on parting. "Okay, Bill," I said. "Tell Ernie and Pete why I am leaving." I walked back to camp.

After breakfast I saw Jim and told him I would not be going on shift. He looked startled at first, then admitted to me that no more money would be forthcoming from Edmonton until the shareholders saw some gold from the channel. Then his attitude changed and he almost shouted, "Ralph, what kind of a damn fool are you to quit now — right when we have just about got everything licked? You know there's gold on the bottom, we can't miss. There must be a million dollars ahead of us."

"I know, Jim," I said, "I hardly slept all night thinking about it. But I'm still leaving on today's plane." He quieted down. "Okay, if that's what you intend to do, then there is nothing more to be said. I still think you are making the biggest mistake of your life."

I soon packed my bedroll and lashed it, with my personal effects, on my pack-board and with my .22 and 6.5 mm rifles started to walk to the Hudson's Bay store at Manson Creek. I had to settle my small account there. Bob Dunsmore accompanied me. He, too, was flying out. We were not sure about getting out at all, because the weather was so wet and stormy with low clouds. The plane was due at Wolverine Lake at two-thirty that afternoon.

After I paid my bill, Jack Copeland, the manager, asked me into his office at the back of the store. He opened the safe and took out a roll of bills. My eyes widened! He counted out sixteen hundred dollars, put it in a buff envelope, licked the gummed flap, and closed it. Calmly he handed it to me. "Would you mind giving this to the manager at the Fort?" he asked. I looked at him, my mouth open. "Oh, you might as well give him this too," he added, handing me a blasting cap box with a taped lid. "Twelve ounces of gold!"

I was speechless for awhile, because it was all done so matter-of-factly. I then said, "How do you know I will give this to the manager — this is the most money I have had in my life?" "Oh, you will," he replied and dismissed the subject. I must admit that deep down somewhere inside of me I felt a warm glow to know that he had such confidence in my honesty.

Bob and I walked to Wolverine Lake in the rain. Once there, it did not take long to get a good fire going, despite the weather, because there was plenty of firewood. We did not talk much. Bob knew the reason I was leaving them.

Soon a native fellow, who was staying in a nearby cabin, joined us. "Your gun?" he asked, pointing to my 6.5 mm Mannlicher, leaned against a big spruce. "Yes," I replied. "What the two trigger for?" he asked. I explained that one was a hair-trigger and picked up the empty rifle to show him how it worked. He took the rifle and set the hair-trigger himself.

"Here, try it." I handed him a shell. He aimed at a whitish rock on the nearest island. The bullet struck dead centre and he seemed surprised. "You want to sell this gun?" "Okay, you can have it for ten dollars," I said. He took out his pocketbook and handed me a ten dollar bill. "I'm going up the mountain and this will be a great caribou gun," he explained. I gave him the rest of the shells and he returned to his cabin.

It was still raining and the clouds were very low down the sides of the mountains. It seemed foolish to wait for the plane under such conditions. Despite this, the plane came in at almost tree-top level, on scheduled time. We helped the pilot tie up and unload the freight for the Hudson's Bay. We covered it with a tarp, then Bob and I climbed aboard.

It was a panicky trip out. Bob sat on the floor because the plane was buffeted by extremely strong crosswinds. Several times I thought it was going to flip over, but the pilot skilfully righted it. We were flying extremely low, but even so quite often we flew into clouds. It was with relief I finally recognized Stuart Lake. It was impossible to land on the open lake because it was much too stormy. The pilot touched down in a sheltered area near the source of Stuart River.

With the motor revving up only sufficiently enough to give the plane forward motion, we started to taxi across the open water toward Huffman's Point. Slowly we edged across, every minute expecting to be capsized by the vicious wind and huge waves. There were some heart-stopping moments as the plane yawed about in the deep troughs.

Suddenly, near the opposite shore and just when we had begun to breath easier, the motor died. Quickly, the pilot dropped onto a pontoon and I climbed down on the other. At the same time, we each grabbed at paddles which had been clipped to the pontoon struts. Seated astride the nose of each pontoon, with our legs dangling in the water, we paddled furiously to make the last few yards to shore. A number of people helped us pull up the plane to safety on the beach.

When it was firmly tied down, Sheldon Luck, the young pilot, turned to me with a grin. "Well, how did you like the trip?" he asked. "Not a bit!" I replied, truthfully. "No, it was not too comfortable at times," he conceded. Bob did not speak. He looked as if he might throw up at any moment. The air trip had been rough enough, even before we landed on the lake. The pilot then went to his small cabin and gave us receipts for the plane fare.

Bob and I stayed in the Fort that night, because I was soaked to the waist. Besides, I had to deliver the money and gold that Jack Copeland had given me. In all the excitement, I had just about forgotten it. It was still stuffed in the inside pocket of my macinaw coat, along with my personal cheques and papers.

At nine o'clock the next morning, I walked over to the Hudson's Bay store and saw Len Murphy, the manager. I knew him slightly, because occasionally we had spoken on my previous visits to the store. I handed him the cash and gold, for which he thanked me. He did not seem the least bit surprised that I should be bringing it from Manson Creek.

I queried, "Well, aren't you going to count it? I prefer that you did, because I saw Jack put sixteen hundred dollars in there." "All right, if it will make you feel better," he said. "Let's go in the office." To this day, I find this little episode still intrigues me. It was their cash and gold, yet it seems I was the only one worrying about it.

On arrival in Vanderhoof, I headed straight for the bank and received cash for my cheques. I breathed a little easier to know they were still good.

I called around to see Chuey and ordered lunch. He joined me after I had finished. I gave him all the news of Manson Creek and the reason why Bill and I separated. I asked his opinion whether or not I had done the right thing by leaving. He nodded his head. "This way you have five hundred dollah for sure." He shrugged, "You stay — you get thousands of dollah — maybe. You do right thing."

I ate supper with the folks at home, because I luckily caught a ride with the Chilco storekeeper. I felt good. This time I had not returned in my usual "broke" condition. I showed them the nugget I had found on that memorable night on Lost Creek and gave them all the story of our efforts on the mining project.

It was hours before sleep finally quieted my excited brain. All the events of the last few days persisted in running through my head in seemingly endless circles. It was a wild jumble of gold, storms, plane rides in which I fell thousands of feet, and mining.

After a couple of days at home, I was beginning to wonder what I should do to pass the time. Already I had begun to miss Bill, Ernie, and the rest of the gang. There was no inkling of events, about to happen, which would not only affect our lives at home, but most of the able-bodied men of the town of Vanderhoof.

On my fourth day at home, Dad drove into Vanderhoof with the Chilco storekeeper, who was the only one among the residents who could afford to license and operate a car. When Dad came home that evening he had a job lined up with a mining company which was to commence operations immediately in the Germansen area. There was a job available for me, too, if I wished to take it.

As Dad described it, they were hiring every male who was capable of working with pick, shovel, and axe, at a fifty cents an hour wage, plus free board. If I wanted a job, all I had to do was to return with him the next day to Vanderhoof, see a Mr. Horace Fraser, and sign up. It was great news indeed, because Germansen was only twenty miles beyond Manson Creek. I was going back to the life I loved!

All was made in readiness that evening for our departure on the morrow. It was easy for me. Most of my personal kit was still assembled, but Dad had to prepare one. The coming winter's supply of fuel was already cut up and stored under cover, so there was no worry on that score. We expected to be away until almost the middle of November if the weather conditions in Germansen were not too severe. As it was now well into September, we expected to be back in six or seven weeks time.

The next day we paid the storekeeper to drive us to Vanderhoof. I immediately presented myself to the engineer-in-charge, Mr. Fraser, who was staying at Day's Hotel. The place was full of men, and it seemed as if this mining company had taken every available room, which indeed they had.

A male stenographer took down all particulars they wanted to know about me, then turned me over to Mr. Fraser. He asked me about my work in Manson Creek, and I could see he was satisfied by my answers. He then asked if I knew of any other fellows who had mining experience who were available. I had to tell him I did not, but that he might find some at Fort St. James.

He then went on to explain just what the situation would be like in Germansen, which he did to all who were desirous of going. This New York company had purchased the hydraulic holdings of Ward and Bauer, and the adjoining Hagberg property on Germansen Creek. They were going to put in a very large hydraulicking operation. But before this could materialize, they had to have a larger water supply.

To obtain this water, they had to dig approximately two and a half miles of ditch-line by the fifteenth of November that year, otherwise the water rights would be lost to another company operating further upstream. If the ditch was completed to a minimum depth of four feet, with at least six inches of water running through it by the deadline, that would be sufficient for this year to hold title. Next year would see machinery brought in to excavate a much larger and longer ditch-line.

In the meantime we would be expected to work ten hours a day, seven days a week, until the job was completed. We would have five meals daily, two in camp and three would be brought out on the job. We would all be driven to Fort St. James, then flown in to Germansen Landing. It was a tremendous boost to the whole economy of the Vanderhoof-Fort St. James area and seemed to be the turning point to more prosperous times.

While none of us had yet met Mr. Charles DeGanahl of White Plains, New York, the multi-millionaire who financed this operation, his personal chauffeur and car were already in Vanderhoof. It was the largest car I had ever seen. There were three rows of seats, the centre ones folding up when not needed. Ten of us rode in comfort that same afternoon, to Fort St. James where rooms were waiting for us at Forfar's Hotel. Dad and I shared the same room.

After a wash and brush-up, I sauntered downstairs to the lobby. A poker game was in progress in one corner, and several kibitzers stood near and watched the game. All were complete strangers to me, but I rightly surmised they had been hired to go to Germansen. They were miners from the Wingdam Mine in the Cariboo.

One extremely big fellow, who was watching the game, was passing a few comments about it. None of the six players said anything to him. This was very unusual, because spectators are supposed to remain mute. However, I soon found out it was not because of the man's bulk the players kept silent, but who he was. He was to be the superintendent of operations at Germansen, second only to the engineer, Mr. Horace Fraser.

This "Bull-o'-the-Woods," Chris Beaton, was one of the last of a breed of men now passed into history. In the earlier years of Canada's growth, his type was common and usually in charge of gangs of labourers whom they quite often ruled by fists of iron. When they roared an order the men jumped to obey. I, among many others, learned the hard way how to deal with the "Bull," as we all called him.

More men came to the hotel every day, and others flew into Germansen when the lake was not too rough for takeoff. We were living like kings, because everything was at the company's expense. We were on the payroll the day we arrived at the Fort. The year 1936 was indeed a memorable one in my life.

I had been at the hotel a week before it was my turn to fly in to Germansen. Four of us took our packs down to Huffman's Point. It was the same plane and pilot who had brought Bob Dunsmore and I from Manson Creek and was now to take me back to Germansen Landing on the Omineca River. As I was climbing into the plane I spoke to the pilot, "I hope you don't treat me so rough this time." He laughed, "No, I don't think you will have to paddle any on this trip." It was a pleasant trip to Germansen, and the landing on the Omineca River was perfect, because for several miles the river was wide, deep and quiet.

On arrival at the Landing, we found we had to walk a couple of miles to the campsite. The camp consisted of one large, and one smaller, log cabin and a number of tents erected as temporary quarters. The cabins were old, but quite habitable and had belonged to the original owners of the property. One cabin had been turned into the cookhouse. On entering I found the cook to be George Ellis, who had given us a meal the year before at the surveyors' camp.

Four to six men were assigned to each tent, and each had to make his own bed from poles and spruce boughs, because no lumber was yet available. We were provided with hammer, nails, and saws. For each tent there was a small air-tight heater. It was rough, but no one minded in the least. We were all glad to be employed at good wages.

One of the foremen was billeted in the same tent as I, and he asked me if I thought I could pick out a good campsite about five miles down trail from the present camp. The new camp was going to be the headquarters for the "ditch crews" who were to start digging the ditch-line. He emphasized that the site should be near good water and not in heavy timber. They did not want to spend time making a clearing.

The next morning after breakfast, packing a lunch and a double-bitted axe, I set off down the trail towards Manson Creek. Near Ah Lock Creek was a perfect place. The wide, open grassy clearing dotted with a few bunches of small willows was a natural site. It was bounded on one side by the creek and at the back by straight lodgepole pine, which could be used for frames for the tents and an easy source of firewood. I decided to look no further, because it was far enough from the other camp to serve the purpose.

The creek was named after an old Chinaman, Ah Lock, who had spent many years washing gold in the Germansen area. It is said that when he finally turned his property over to a fellow named Albin Hagberg, in the early nineteen-thirties, he had something like fifty thousand dollars in placer gold. The company had, in turn, purchased this property from Hagberg and planned on hydraulic mining along the benches above Germansen Creek — hence the reason for the ditch-line and a larger water supply.

After eating lunch, I returned to camp to report to the foreman Jack Adams what I considered a perfect campsite near the trail-crossing at Ah Lock Creek.

Six of us started out the next day with two pack horses laden with tents, tools, and grub. We were going to stay there, and our job was to fix up a tent for ourselves, then select the best site for the cook tents to be erected. An extra large cook tent was made by joining up two twenty-foot tents. Only the packer and his horses returned to the main camp that evening, and the next day they brought in more supplies. More men came every day, and soon we had a row of tents housing at least fifty men.

It was a happy, busy camp. Soon everything was finished, and we could start on the real job of digging. The ditch-line had been surveyed. Each man — complete with pick and shovel — was given a twenty-foot section to dig. Some were more adept than others, because the men were from all professions and trades. As each man completed his section, he moved up to the head of the line, and he had to take the first open section, no matter what type of ground. Extra hard or difficult digging usually found a miner sent back to help the digger complete his section, so he could keep up with the main body of workers. We started at seven a.m. and were back in camp at six p.m. There was a half hour break at noon, with two fifteen minute breaks in the morning and afternoon. There was food to eat, of the best quality, every time we stopped. It was one of the happiest camps I have ever seen anywhere.

Naturally, among such a cross section of human personalities, characteristics were brought to the surface as we became better acquainted. Three young fellows, in particular, would be liable to put on an impromptu show any time they happened to be together after supper. They became known to the rest of us as the "Three Clowns," because they could keep the camp in stitches with their antics.

One was an ex-Hudson's Bay clerk, another a miner from Wingdam, who had wrestled to the semi-finals in the All Canada Championship Contest, and the third was an ex-farm boy from Vanderhoof.

The gags, jokes, and mimicry flew so fast when they got together the rest of us would be almost helpless from laughter. The ex-clerk's specialty was dancing. He could mimic a ballerina down to the last movement of the hands and torso, and could out-do the Cossacks when it came to performing their type of dance. All three were first class athletes and sometimes put on a show on the parallel bars, which they had rigged up. Had they lived in a different decade, they would not have had to waste their talents on digging ditches.

Another character was "Squeaky" McDermott. Squeaky, in his own way, was as funny as anyone without intending to be. He was a big man with a deep, gruff voice when he spoke naturally. He loved to tell and laugh at his own jokes. He would start the story in his normal voice, but as he was getting to the punch line his voice was gradually rising in pitch until, at the climax, he was as shrill as a little girl. Of course everyone roared with laughter, not so much at the joke, but at the big change in Squeaky's voice. Sometimes he was so shrill he had a hard time finding enough breath to finish his story. The whole camp knew when he was telling one of his jokes, because his audience would start laughing before he could finish it. But he never seemed to catch on why they were laughing.

The month of October that year favoured us with ideal weather, cold frosty mornings with blue, sunny skies until sundown. Only one day of rain the whole month and no snow at all. The ditch-line was being rapidly completed, and if nothing untoward happened, the deadline would easily be met.

I often wondered how Bill and the rest of the gang were making out on Lost Creek. There was no story of any big strike being made there. I decided I would ask for leave of absence on the last Sunday of October, so I could walk over to Manson and find out. I met Bill and Ernie at the Hudson's Bay store, because they too had taken a day off. That was very fortunate for me and saved an extra three miles walk to Lost Creek. They had not reached the bottom of the channel!

Jim had miscalculated and the tunnel was punched through the rim too high. They had tried to sink another shaft from the tunnel, but were beaten by more water and bad air.

Jim was in Edmonton, trying to raise more money to sink another shaft from the surface down to bedrock in the centre of the channel. To do this he would have to have a steam donkey to hoist the overburden and paydirt up the shaft, and a compressor to supply air for ventilation, and run the pumps at the new contemplated depth of one hundred feet. In the meantime all the men were cutting timbers and lagging for the new shaft, which was already in the initial stage.

A small amount of gold had been taken out of the first shaft, but they would have to find true bedrock before they could hope for anything better. Jim had told them there was no money in the bank to meet their cheques, and the only hope was to stay with the job until bedrock was reached. The Hudson's Bay gave them credit for the few personal items they needed.

I was genuinely sorry to hear how things had turned out, because this made it two years in a row Bill had worked for nothing. However, he was still confident that everything would turn out all right in the end. It was a very tired person who finally made it back to bed in the early hours of the next morning. I had walked almost twenty-eight miles on the round trip, much of it by the light of a flashlight.

As November began, it was a certainty the ditch would be completed before the deadline. There were but a few days work to finish it. On the fifth of the month, Mr. Horace Fraser, accompanied by Bull Beaton, walked down from the main camp and we were paid off, each man receiving two extra days pay.

Mr. Fraser gave a short speech, thanking us for completing the job ahead of schedule. He told us that twenty-six men would walk to the C. M. & S. camp on Slate Creek, where we would be bedded down for the night. We were to wait there until Perison's truck came in to pick us up for the balance of the trip to Fort St. James.

Work had been done improving and widening the Baldy road, and a few trips had been made into Manson Creek during the summer and fall by truck. The first, ever, gasoline driven vehicle to arrive in Manson Creek was a truck driven by Harold Perison, which arrived at the Hudson's Bay store on July 27, 1936.

Dad and I were among the first bunch of twenty-six men to leave, because our names had been selected alphabetically. It was snowing lightly when we all started down the trail to Manson Creek, packing our bedrolls. It was the first snow of the winter and the day was quite cold. Everyone seemed in good shape, and the eleven-mile hike to Slate Creek was easy.

On arrival at the mine we were allotted cabins by the same man Bill and I had met the year before. We never saw our old "friend" Ogilvie. It was hard to imagine Ogilvie providing sleeping accommodation and meals to strange men. I can only conclude it was done because Charles DeGanahl was an extremely wealthy man and head of a number of worldwide mining companies.

It snowed three inches that night, and we awoke the next morning to bright moonlight and twelve degrees below zero. We had only just completed the ditch in time, before winter set in. Breakfast was at five a.m. and we were on our way by six, because Harold Perison was already at Slate Creek.

Twenty-six men with packs was quite a load for the truck, and the stake body was open to the weather. We crawled in compound low gear, climbing the slopes of Baldy Mountain, and the snowfall did nothing to help the traction.

On the last steep grade before reaching the summit, the wheels spun out, and we could make no more headway. Everyone but the driver and his swamper jumped out and tried to push, but there was not room for everyone. The swamper then got out and tied two long ropes to the front bumper. Then, with about four pushing, the rest pulling on the ropes and the truck using its power, we had no difficulty making the severe pitch to the summit.

Progress was very slow, little more than a crawl, because the "road" was extremely rough and rocky. Despite the cold and the conditions, we were in good spirits, because some of the boys kept up a stream of wisecracks and anecdotes.

We were near Gillis' Grave when old Sam Heppner, the second cook, who could spin a great yarn, spoke up and said, "I think I'll go and join old Gillis on the hill, as he can't be any colder than I am." As he said this, he stood up to look in the direction of the grave and did not notice a "sweeper" hanging over the road. The limb struck him over the nose and beneath his eye and put a deep gash near the cheekbone. Whether old Sam took this as a sign or omen, I don't know, but he was very quiet after the incident and had a real "shiner" by the time he arrived at the Fort.

That night we stayed at Twelve Mile Cabins, where Bill, Les, Frenchy, and I had rested when we walked out. Ed Kohse and his wife were occupying one of the cabins, which belonged to him. We all bedded down wherever we could on the floors of the cabins. They were as hospitable as possible under the circumstances and did not seem the least perturbed that a large number of men had dropped in on them, unexpectedly, at night.

They were German people, and the walls of the cabin had at least a dozen pictures of Adolph Hitler in various military poses. The way Ed spoke about him, he sincerely believed that Hitler would be the saviour of Germany. He changed his mind sometime later, when some of his own relatives were executed and others jailed in one of Hitler's infamous "purges."

Despite the unusual bed, I slept very well and hated to be aroused again at five a.m. The wash in ice-cold water from the creek removed the heaviness from my eyes, and breakfast of coffee, bacon and beans, and hot cakes was not hard to take.

The truck, with its load of humanity, was on its way by six-thirty. The best sections of the road found us speeding at around fifteen miles per hour, but this was maintained for only a few minutes at a time. We stopped at the Nation River for lunch and to stretch our legs. It was chilly! — around the zero mark.

Harold Perison, the driver, figured we would make Fort St. James between seven and eight o'clock. The burnt section through Giddegingla was tough, because many ice-covered waterholes were encountered. In addition, there were many sweepers from the overhanging burnt pines.

As darkness began, the talk and laughter gradually ceased. We were all huddled together for warmth, our bodies rolling in unison with the sway of the truck, as it ground over the bumpy road. Stiff with cold, we finally pulled up in front of Forfar's Hotel. It had been a long day!

It was good to be back home again and to take things a little easier. For the first time in many years, I was in the happy condition known as being "stakey." I had already decided I would take a trip back to the Old Country for Christmas. I suppose most immigrants dream of that, whatever their country of origin, and I was no exception. However, I considered I had plenty of time before arranging for the transportation of rail and boat travel.

I spent several days hunting in the Chilco area with a borrowed 30-30 rifle. Big game was plentiful, and I saw a number of deer and moose, but seemed unable to be in the right place at the right time to get a good shot at them. However, I did bag quite a few willow grouse and spruce hen with my .22, closer to home.

The days passed pleasantly enough, and during the first week in December, I went to Vanderhoof to book my passage to the Old Country. When arranging the details, the station agent casually asked me if my passport was in order. What a jolt that gave me! The plain truth was that I had completely forgotten to obtain one!

When I asked him how long it would take to get one from Ottawa, he said probably two or three weeks. That meant I could not make it over to Europe for Christmas. It was a big disappointment, but only I was to blame. What an idiot I was!

I walked back to Chuey's restaurant to try and figure things out over a piece of his famous pie and coffee. Gradually I began to reason that it was not so terrible after all. I was young and had the promise of a season's work with DeGanahl's at Germansen next year. I would save my money and go to the Old Country for Christmas next year. It was as simple as that!

As Robbie Burns once said, "The best laid schemes o' mice and men — " It was exactly ten years later when I set foot in the land of my birth!

On arrival at home that evening I was pleasantly surprised to find Bill visiting the folks. He had made the trip by plane to Fort St. James, the first trip on skis after the lakes froze over. I was sure glad to see him again and to know he was staying in Chilco for the winter.

He filled me in on the latest developments at the mine on Lost Creek. Jim had returned from Edmonton with enough money to continue the new shaft sinking during the winter. The company was going to provide him with a steam donkey engine and a large compressor which would supply air for the underground work.

In addition, jackhammers and air-picks would replace the conventional hand tools. It sounded very good, and it was unfortunate the company had not put in this equipment at the beginning. The only sour note was that there was no money for wages. This would have to come out of the gold on bedrock.

Bill decided he would stay in Chilco for the winter and return to Lost Creek in the spring, because he would have to go back to make sure he received the wages due him. Before leaving, Jim had given him enough money to cover the cost of his plane fare and twenty-five dollars extra.

I told him I had abandoned the idea of making the trip overseas for another year, so we decided to obtain a timber limit to cut ties. One of Bill's friends of his school days joined us to make it a trio. "Big" John Reynolds was younger than we, but a tall, rangy fellow of six feet, four inches. We spent some time constructing a three-room cabin on the timber sale we obtained. It was made of lodgepole pine, and everything but the logs was salvaged material from abandoned homesteads.

Each of us had a five hundred tie contract with George Ogston of Vanderhoof. John's sister Pearl did the cooking for us. We spent a happy, carefree winter in the tie camp, and our leisure hours were passed either playing cribbage for matches or practising on our musical instruments.

John was quite adept on a small chromatic accordion he owned, but he thought he would like to have a piano-accordion. He obtained one through one of the mail-order houses, but found the method of playing entirely different and could make very little progress. As a schoolboy I had taken piano lessons for two years, but had not continued. Now, I found some of the knowledge quickly returned. In very little time I was able to play well enough to get by. In addition, we had a Spanish guitar, a mandolin-banjo, and a banjo-uke. We practised several times a week and always played for any dances held locally.

The Second Gold Rush

February of 1937 was one of the coldest on record. The reason I remember it so clearly is that we agreed to stay indoors if it was twenty below zero or lower at eight o'clock in the morning. Only two mornings the whole month was it above that temperature and one of these was the last day of the month. The three of us would stay up playing cribbage all night, keeping up the fire, while the mercury slid down between forty and fifty below. We would eat a big feed of "mush" at midnight. In the daytime we would cut more firewood, then catch up on some sleep, while Pearl kept the fire going and cooked.

There was a dance to be held in the Legion Hall in Vanderhoof on the night of the twenty-seventh, and the three of us decided to go, because Bill and John wished to draw some money against the number of ties they had already cut. That night, or rather early morning, when the dance ended, it was a cool thirty-two below zero when we walked back to our room in Day's Hotel.

When I awoke around ten a.m. the sun was shining and I thought I could hear water running. I thought it must be my imagination, until I looked out of the window. The water was running off the roof! A Chinook wind was blowing and the temperature was fifty-four above. Never before, nor since, have I seen a temperature change of eighty-six degrees in just a few hours. We carried our heavy mackinaw coats over our arms, walking back to Chilco that afternoon of the last day of February 1937.

The remainder of the winter was pleasant and mild, and soon we started to think about returning to the mining area. Bill left around the middle of April. From Fort St. James he flew to Manson Creek to rejoin the rest of the crew who had remained at Lost Creek.

I left for Fort St. James during the first week of May. That was a mistake, because the plane service was discontinued until Stuart Lake was free of ice. I sent a message to the mine at Germansen, via radio, because DeGanahl's had a Morse operator stationed in Fort St. James. The reply from Germansen verified that a job was open for me on arrival there. I decided to walk, instead of waiting for the plane to return from Edmonton where it had gone to be fitted with pontoons for the summer season.

Deciding to walk was the second mistake! I hired a car to take me the first five or six miles north of the Fort, then I had to walk because the road was too soft for further car travel.

That evening I set up camp at thirty-two miles north. It snowed a couple of inches during the night, but I decided to push on because there was no chance the snow would remain.

The second evening found me at Horseshoe Lake, some fifty miles on my way to Germansen. It was cold and looked like more snow or rain, so I decided to stay at one of the trappers' cabins there. There was no lock on the outside of the door, but it was barred from the inside. It did not take long to discover the trapper's method of opening the door, so I slept on one of the two bunks inside. There was a small heater, so I spent a comfortable night.

I was preparing breakfast next morning when I suddenly began to feel nauseated. I could not eat anything I had prepared. It was not wise to continue the journey the way I felt, because there was still ninety miles to walk before reaching Germansen. My best policy would be to go back to the Fort and wait for the plane to return.

It was a tough day! I suffered from a raging thirst, but every time I drank water I would immediately vomit, and the thirst would return. Despite the pack on my back and a burning fever, I kept walking south towards Fort St. James. I ate nothing, but late in the afternoon began to feel a little better. I decided to try another drink of water, and this time I did not vomit.

I gradually began to feel more normal, and by the time I got back to twenty-four mile I was hungry. Even before setting up the canvas fly for the night, I lit a fire and cooked a little bacon, which I ate with bread. Only after a good mug of tea, did I prepare camp. I was completely back to normal next morning when I headed on the last lap towards Fort St. James.

A few miles down the road there was a truck bogged in a hole. No one was around, but there was evidence someone had been working on it. Further on I met Harold Perison and his helper walking towards the bogged truck. They had a new axle with them.

Harold told me he had managed to drive his smaller one-ton truck as far as sixteen miles north of the Fort, with the spare axle. He asked me to drive the one-ton back to the Fort, because they were going to bring out the bigger truck once they had replaced the broken axle. I was only too happy to oblige, because it saved me quite a long walk.

There were some bad sections to cross, but I got out of the cab and looked them over carefully before deciding whether I should hit them at high speed or use the lowest gear and just crawl. It was good to see Stuart Lake again from the hill just north of the town.

For almost a week I stayed with a number of fellows in a small cabin back of the Hudson's Bay store. I had money with me and still more in the bank in Vanderhoof, so just loafed around. There was still no sign of the plane.

One of the boys at the cabin had a beautiful piano-accordion, which he wanted to sell for eighty dollars, because he was going with a pack train on a prospecting trip. I played it often and decided in my own mind I would buy it before he left, although I did not mention it to him. It was not to be. It was destroyed in the fire which levelled the cabin in a matter of twenty minutes.

How the fire started, no one could explain. I was helping repair a car which had broken down on the other side of town when it happened, and by the time I got back it was impossible to approach the burning building.

We all lost everything but the clothes we were wearing. In addition, the loss of the building was itself a tragedy, because it was part of the old original trading post. I was fortunate to be in the position to buy a new outfit, but some of the boys were really in a bad way. I know some of them were helped by the manager of the Hudson's Bay store, Len Murphy. After the fire I moved down to Huffman's Point and stayed in one of the small cabins there.

The plane returned from Edmonton, and I went to see Sheldon Luck, the pilot, to ask when he was making a flight to Germansen. He could not give a definite date, but promised to inform me when he was sure. It was several days before I finally flew in with him to Germansen.

On arrival there I was put in a crew which was to open up No. 2 Pit. All the pits or hydraulic operations were numbered. No. 1 Pit was at the main camp on the old Ward and Bauer leases. Plans were in progress to build a huge ditch and flume to tap Germansen Lake, approximately twelve miles from the main camp. When completed it would supply one hundred and fifty cubic feet of water per second to the various operations which were planned. It was a tremendous and bold undertaking, and needed the backing of a millionaire of Charles DeGanahl's stature to bring it to completion.

Power shovels were brought in with dragline booms, a couple of RD7 bulldozers, numerous trucks, and power units. At first acetylene flares were used for pit illumination. Later electrical generators were installed, and all camps and operations were supplied with electricity. Until the huge project was completed, we had to carry on with the amount of water available from existing ditch-lines.

The DeGanahl operations were known as Germansen Ventures Ltd., which in turn was a subsidiary of Ventures Exploration (East Africa) Ltd. How many other mines and companies Charles De-Ganahl owned was not known to me, but I believe he controlled Fleetwings Aircraft Corporation in the U.S.A. We were to see much of him at a later date in Germansen.

The foreman in charge of No. 2 Pit construction was Frank Chapuis, known to all of us as "Chappie." He, in turn, was under the authority of Chris Beaton, who stayed at the main camp. We were happy with this arrangement, because already Beaton was getting a reputation for being a hard man to work for. The less we saw of him the better we liked it.

We had our own cookhouse at No. 2 Camp, and tents for sleeping quarters where about a dozen of us were billeted. The work proceeded steadily, and we completed the whole construction from flume, penstock, pipeline, to monitors. I learned much from Chappie, because he was a first class hydraulic man, besides being a good foreman, whom we all liked and respected.

Once the water was turned on, I was given the job of sluice-tender, more familiarly known as a "rock-puller." My job was to hook the big rocks that were pushed into the sluice boxes by the rush of water from the monitors and keep them moving through the boxes until they were washed to the tailing dumps.

Many yards of gravel were passing through the sluices every minute, so it was imperative to prevent the large boulders from causing blockages in this flow. Occasionally it became impossible to prevent a jam, then I would signal the monitor man not to wash down more gravel until the boxes were cleared. It was enjoyable work and the time passed very quickly.

I would also take my turn, under the guidance of Chappie, in operating one of the pit monitors. This fascinated me completely, because it was amazing the way gravel and boulders could be moved by the proper application of water under pressure. The monitors were small — compared to the monsters which were later installed in No. 1 Pit after the big ditch was completed — but they looked big to me at the time. We used the three inch for cutting the gravel banks and the four inch nozzles for washing through the sluice boxes.

The weeks passed quickly and I became more experienced in all phases of placer hydraulics. In addition, my bank balance was steadily growing, because I never drew any pay, but asked the company to send my pay cheques directly to the bank. Occasionally I would walk to No. 1 Camp in the evenings and join in the poker game which seemed to be continually running, because the bulk of the men were in camp there.

Charles DeGanahl had arrived from New York with his son Frank. They were very big men — as big as Chris Beaton. There was no mistaking the respect in which Charles DeGanahl was held. Even his own son addressed him as "sir." Despite this, he was approachable by anyone and was liable to question any employee about the work on which he happened to be employed.

Not so with his son Frank. He held himself aloof from all, and it was soon evident that he thought the whole Germansen operation nothing but a childish whim on the part of his father. Of course he dare not tell his father this.

I had occasion to witness a little incident during the clean-up of the sluice boxes in No. 2 Pit. Frank DeGanahl, along with Chris Beaton, had arrived to see the clean-up. When completed, there were two tobacco cans full of gold, which Beaton took over to show Frank DeGanahl. "Pretty good, eh, Mr. DeGanahl?" said Chris Beaton. Frank turned away in disgust. "Umph," he grunted. "If one of my niggers in Africa did not bring me this much every day, I would fire him." Such was his opinion of our efforts in Canada. However, his opinions counted for nothing while his father was alive, because the old man dearly loved to spend the summers in Germansen, away from the hurly-burly of New York.

The main camp was growing in size every day. A sawmill and planer had been set up at Germansen Landing, because millions of feet of lumber were needed to complete the flume section of the big ditch-line. In addition, many houses and cabins were constructed to house the ever-growing number of employees. Scores of men came in from the prairies, because they had heard of the good wages being paid.

I was quite satisfied to be in the smaller camp at No. 2 Pit with Chappie and the rest of our crew. Our operation seemed to run so smoothly, compared to the many different projects being under construction at the main camp.

To pass away some of the long evenings I still walked occasionally to No. 1 Camp to sit in on the poker game. It was this little habit of mine which eventually brought me into contact with the Bull-o'-the-Woods, Chris Beaton. I was sitting in the card game one night when he came stamping into the room. It was plain to see he was in his usual bad temper, but I was very surprised when he addressed me, "I hear you are an underground miner." When I acknowledged I had some experience, he went on, "Well, you start in the morning in the gopher-hole." (The gopher-hole was a four feet square exploratory drift in one of the channels.)

"But I want to stay with Chappie," I protested. "The hell with Chappie!" he roared, "You be here at eight o'clock in the morning." I could feel my face begin to turn red. "All right, but you pay me underground wages," I said. "The hell I will — it's an easy job," he said as he turned to the door. "My daughter could do it," he added.

I lost my temper. "Well, bring your daughter at eight in the morning." He turned back from the door and started to use the filthy language for which he was noted. Most of the men had to take it, because jobs were so scarce, and no doubt I would have had to take it a couple of years earlier.

Now things were different, because I was quite "stakey." I interrupted his flow of profanity. "You can make out my time right now," I said. That stopped him and he banged the door as he left the room.

I was upset and could not settle down in the card game after that, so walked back to No. 2 Camp. I explained to Chappie what had happened at No. 1 Camp, and that I was leaving the next day. If I did not leave, I knew Beaton would "ride" me unmercifully, because he did it to all who took his abuse.

I felt a little despondent when I set out to get my cheque at the office at the main camp the next morning. All day I sat on a wooden bench outside the building, but no pay cheque. The next day I was back again. I went in the cookhouse for the midday meal with the rest of the crew.

Coming outside after the meal I met Beaton and the engineer-in-charge. "What are you doing here?" Beaton asked in a surprised voice. I knew he was putting on an act for his superior's benefit. "You know I am waiting for my time."

He waved his arm in the general direction of No. 2 Camp. "Oh, go on back! Go on back with Chappie," he said. "No, thanks, I'm staying here until I get my pay," I replied.

The engineer Mr. Eassie, who had recently replaced the former engineer, gave me a searching look, but said nothing. They entered the cookhouse and I took up my vigil on the wooden bench beside the office. Late the next day, making three days in all, one of the clerks finally handed me my time statement and pay cheque.

I stayed at No. 2 Camp that night, and next morning, with my bedroll on the pack-board, headed down trail to Manson Creek. I was sorry to leave Chappie and the rest, but was determined I was going to take nothing from Chris Beaton. I had obtained a solid background of general hydraulics under Chappie's tuition, and it was to be of benefit to me in the years ahead.

It was almost the end of July when I headed for Manson. I wanted to see Bill, Ernie, and the rest of the boys on Lost Creek. Manson Creek settlement was an amazing sight near the Hudson's Bay store. Scores of small tents, lean-tos, and canvas flies were set up among the small jack pines. Another store had been built on the opposite bank of Slate Creek, and several other cabins were in various stages of construction.

Men were everywhere! It was fantastic! Here was the second gold rush to Manson at its height. A few individuals were well equipped and obviously had means, but the vast majority had arrived with nothing but the bare necessities.

The bars and benches of the creeks were swarming with snipers, all intent on obtaining enough gold to survive. How some of them made enough to eat is hard to explain, although it was a good year for berries, grouse, and caribou. Not all were in a position to obtain meat, because many did not possess rifles.

In addition to the snipers, many men were employed by the C. M. & S. operation on Slate Creek, the Dunsmore mine on Lost Creek, the Bert MacDonald placers at the mouth of Lost Creek, and the Bob Adams operation on Manson Creek.

Several smaller concerns also were active. Some were legitimate, but others were not. It was inevitable that some of the "get-rich-quick" boys and shysters would find their way to Manson Creek.

One, at least, of these shysters was taken out by the Fort St. James police and given a jail term.

On the other hand, it was incredible that the crime rate was so low. Not a single crime of violence was committed! No one was shot, neither did anyone get his head battered. There were a few isolated cases of thievery, but these were usually of food, and no doubt the result of hunger pangs. Some of the boys died and others were injured, but none from the violence of his neighbour.

There was very little drinking, for the reason that few had money to spare for liquor. The hard cases, who had to have alcohol, usually obtained it by buying lemon and vanilla extract or liniment from the stores. This they would mix with fruit juices to concoct a "witches cocktail." It was these cocktails which led to the death of one man.

He had been on a bender for three days with a couple of his friends, when he suddenly keeled over. He was dead before he hit the floor, and the Bob Adams operation was minus a good blacksmith.

Another character was "Rough-house Johnny" or "Seven-day" MacDougal. A short, stocky Irishman in his middle fifties, he had acquired his nickname as a young man. It was said he never kept a job more than seven days. Sometimes he quit, but more often he was fired for fighting. I visited Johnny often, as he lived alone in a tiny cabin on the banks of Slate Creek. Sometimes I would play a borrowed accordion for him, because he loved to lie on his bunk, hands behind his head, and listen. His two favourites were "When Irish Eyes Are Smiling" and "Chapel In The Moonlight." I never found the source of his income, nor, I believe, did anyone else. He never worked, yet he always had enough money to buy the plain necessities of life. His fighting days over, he lived a tranquil life.

Among such a cross section of humanity there were many outstanding and skilful men, because the depression years had forced many to try and make a living in the Manson gold fields.

Naturally, on my return to Manson from Germansen, I first visited Bill and the boys on Lost Creek to see how they were doing. Jim was very affable and invited me to look over the underground workings.

A completely new camp had been constructed. More than twenty men were employed underground. In addition, a boiler room which housed the upright steam boiler and air compressors had been completed. It was an impressive sight, with the pit headgear over the finished shaft. The new shaft had hit the centre of the buried channel.

I was provided with an acetylene lamp, then Jim and I were lowered in the cage to the bottom of the shaft. It was ninety-seven feet to bedrock, where a ten foot deep sump had been made to collect the drainage for pumping to the surface. From the bottom of the shaft, mine-car rails had been laid on bedrock to the working faces of the drifts and crosscuts.

Both Bill and Ernie were on shift when I arrived and were surprised to see me. We shook hands, almost one hundred feet below the surface. Bill was using an air-pick on the gravel face, while Ernie drilled holes with a jackhammer in bedrock.

This was done not only to level the rock floor, but to lift at least two feet of bedrock by blasting. Much gold was in the cracks and crevices. The channel was very rich in places, and Ernie told me of cleaning out a small cross-crevice in bedrock. When the paydirt was panned, it yielded one hundred and five dollars from less than two shovelfuls of dirt.

I thought I had made a very bad error in leaving the mine, until I spoke privately with Bill and Ernie later that night. They were now receiving full wages from the gold being mined, but had received none of the back pay due them. There was a large payroll to meet at the mine, plus many debts to be paid off. They did not know where the surplus gold was going, but suspected some of it was being "high-graded."

Jim had promised them full restitution once everything was paid off for equipment, but it did not turn out that way, because Jim did not have the final say. An engineer was sent from Edmonton and placed in seniority. Despite this, I was glad to know they were now receiving regular pay and that the channel was yielding some of its wealth. It was fitting their faith had been justified, even if they never received payment for much of the hard work previously done. Billy Steele's story was true! There was much gold in the old buried channel, and to this day much more is still buried there. Someday it will be recovered!

Jim invited me to return and work at the mine, but I was not intrigued with the idea of working underground anymore. I planned on doing a little sniping somewhere on Manson Creek. Skookum Davidson said I could make use of his tent, if I would watch his cache of horse feed built nearby. It was a big tent, set up on log walls about four tiers high. It contained a table, wood stove, and three homemade bunks. I was very comfortable.

For a week or more I wandered up and down Manson Creek, with gold pan and shovel, testing the bars and benches which were not occupied by other snipers. I was in no hurry. "Colours," or fine gold could be obtained almost anywhere, but I was interested in mining coarser stuff.

A couple of hundred yards upstream from the tent, two men were working a bar. They were both wearing hip-waders and digging under two feet of water. Despite this, they were averaging almost an ounce of fine gold a day, which was big pay at that time. I became quite friendly with them, and several times did some sample panning for them. The paydirt carried literally thousands of colours to the pan.

Suddenly an idea struck me. There was a similar bar almost opposite my tent, on the inbow of the creek. Only the top foot or so was above water level, and this was pitted with holes where other snipers had tested the gravels, only to conclude there was nothing worthwhile. I reasoned if I started about a hundred feet downstream where the bar petered out, I could dig a drainage ditch and so be able to get down several feet in the bar gravel at its widest point without water seepage bothering me.

It worked beautifully. As the ditch progressed, it got deeper and the gold better in the bottom gravels. By the time the widest point of the bar was reached, I was down almost four feet below the water level of the creek, with weeks of digging ahead of me.

I purchased several hundred feet of rough boards from the Bob Adams operation and set about building sluice boxes and riffles to catch the gold. Several more days were needed to construct a wing-dam in the creek and set up the flume and sluice boxes, but at last came the day when I started to "shovel-in."

I cleaned up that evening and took the gold to the store to be weighed. I had made seven dollars and thirty cents! This was almost twice the wages paid at the various mines. It was enjoyable healthy work and I usually started to shovel-in around seven a.m. I cleaned the riffles about four p.m. each day. My best day's pay was almost fifteen dollars, and my poorest was four. I had averaged about nine dollars a day for twenty-five days before the gold began to peter out, because the bar gravel was almost finished.

It was at this time I met a fellow who was to figure in one of the north country's bizarre mysteries. I came upon him as he was trying to fry a couple of rashers of bacon over an open campfire, in a heavy rainstorm. I had been visiting some of the snipers most of the day, because the weather was wet and stormy, and had not done any digging. He was a stranger and had just set up a canvas fly. He was shivering as he tried to cook over the smoky fire. I invited him to my tent to cook his meal on the stove. He brought a small slab of bacon with him. It was all the food he had!

It took only a few minutes to light the fire in the stove and make the tent warm and comfortable. I put a can of sausages, also eggs, and bannock on the table and told him to help himself. He did just that — he cleaned up everything, except some of his bacon. He was the hungriest fellow I had ever met! It was all the more remarkable because he was so short and skinny.

After the meal he told me his name was Art Evans. He had done a little trapping, but no placer mining of any kind. I knew he was flat broke, because it was obvious from his meagre outfit. He did not volunteer any information about where he came from, and I did not ask. I invited him to share the tent with me, because there were two empty bunks. Sometimes I almost regretted being so impulsive because the amount of grub he could consume at a sitting was phenomenal.

Finally, I let him take over the bar. I was now working towards the bench and making between two and three dollars a day. I figured he could also keep himself on that amount.

A new store manager had now replaced Jack Copeland at the Hudson's Bay post. His name was Roy Cunningham. We quickly became friendly, and I often visited him in the cabin behind the store, where he lived, because he wished to know about the various mining operations being carried on. From this information, he could order goods to fill the needs of the different types of mining. Because I was not digging, I often helped him in the store, just to pass the time.

Art was still plugging away at what was left of the bar, but it was soon to end. One day Skookum Davidson returned and said he needed his tent, so we had to leave. Art set up his canvas fly again, and I moved to a tent further downstream. It was now getting late in the fall, and one day Art pulled up stakes and was gone.

I never saw him again, but years later I read of the mystery of his death. The first account was in the official Provincial Police gazette called *The Shoulder Strap*. The second account was in one of the detective magazines published in the United States. The official version had it that Art Evans and a partner had left Hazelton during the winter to start trapping. When they did not return by spring, a search was conducted by the Provincial Police.

The first to be discovered was Evans' partner. How he died was not explained, but he was found lying with head and shoulders in what had been the campfire. The fire must have been very hot, because the head was partly consumed.

Evans' body was found several miles away, also near an extinct campfire. From the evidence, it was known he had lived longer than his partner. The body was terribly emaciated, and the police said he was wearing several suits of heavy underwear, as well as heavy outer clothing. He had a number of pelts with him and carcasses of the skinned animals were found nearby.

If he had died of starvation, which the police thought, why had he not cooked and eaten the carcasses? Why, also, had he and his partner separated? No mention of foul play was printed in the official version, but the United States story said that foul play was suspected by the police. The story also said Evans was suspected of killing his partner and trying to destroy the evidence by burning. Yet even this version could not explain what Evans hoped to gain by eliminating his partner, because their fur catch did not have a large value.

After living and working with Evans I find it hard to believe he could commit murder. My own theory is that Evans came back from a trip to find his partner already dead. He could have suffered a heart attack and fallen in the fire. Because it was the middle of winter, there was no chance for him to bury the body.

I believe he was on his way out when he, himself, died. Not from malnutrition as such, but from some other cause. There was obviously something wrong with him, because no ordinary person could consume so much food, yet remain so thin and run-down. The whole story may never be known, because there were other facts which were equally puzzling. It cannot be entirely ruled out that a third party may have been responsible for at least one of the deaths.

As the nights grew colder and longer, many of the snipers began to leave Manson. Gradually the tents disappeared, and the men who remained were all housed in log cabins.

I debated with myself whether I should winter in Manson or return to Chilco. For some reason, I had lost all desire to make a trip back to Europe, because I loved the free life of the placer fields. I had obtained a newfound confidence in my ability to survive, no matter how grim the conditions appeared.

As in most mining camps, card games were the main form of relaxation, and Manson Creek was no exception. A poker game was liable to begin at any cabin where enough miners were gathered. Quite often a game would be in progress all Saturday and Sunday in the cabin behind the Hudson's Bay store. Roy Cunningham, the manager, did not play, but enjoyed watching at times. Both cash and gold were used as stakes, the gold being in small glass bottles with the value printed on a label.

One old fellow, Hughie MacLean, was always there with his bottle of gold. He made me wonder how he could sit there for a couple of days without sleeping. He ate very little, but drank lots of coffee. He was seventy-two years of age.

Another steady was "Red" Cotton. Red had been in Manson all summer, barely eking a living on the bars and benches. He was a peculiar type of fellow, who loved to use big words. He would never use a single syllable word if he could find one which had several syllables and meant the same thing. Sometimes he would use them incorrectly, with the result most of the miners thought him to be a stuffed shirt or trying to impress them with a superior education. Consequently, he was something of an outcast.

The card players hated to see him sit in a poker game, because he played his cards, as the saying goes, "close to his chest." He would take several minutes to decide whether he should call a dollar bet. He always carried a woman's purse at the game, in which he kept his few dollars, but no one made any wisecracks about it. They respected his iron fists. He had once hit a man who had made an uncomplimentary remark about his person. One blow had laid the unwise miner cold for twenty minutes.

Around October, 'flu hit the settlement hard. One of the first to go down was Roy Cunningham. He asked me if I would keep an eye on the store for a few days, because he was confined to bed. Dozens of the miners were sick.

Sheldon Luck with Norseman plane.

Ford Tri-Motor — largest seaplane in Canada, 1938. Sheldon Luck, pilot.

Crack-up at Slate Creek.

Russ Baker flying low-wing Junkers. Coming in to Germansen Landing, Omineca River.

Flume construction, Germansen Canyon, 1937.

Impounding dam at outlet of Germansen Lake, 1937.

Water diversion dam on water supply system to hydraulic mine at Ward and Bauer pit — Germansen Ventures Ltd., 1937.

Germansen No. 1 pit. Tony Pini sidesaddle on the nine-inch monitor.

Germansen No. 2 pit in operation. Two four-inch monitors being used.

Clean-up operations — sweeping down.

Cec Jonas cleaning bedrock in the No. 1 pit.

Exploratory drift in No. 3 pit, Germansen Ventures.

Final clean-up and gold!

After a couple of days, I moved my bed into the back of the store, because Roy was getting worse and needed some help. I asked if I should send out word via the radio at Germansen, for someone to come from Fort St. James to run the store. He would not let me do this, because he was sure he would soon recover. I spent all my time between Roy's cabin and the store. He gave me a list of names who were considered good credit risks, because many of the miners were broke.

For three weeks we carried on, and as far as I was concerned, I found the store work most interesting. I purchased quite a lot of gold, especially from the mine on Lost Creek. Each night I would check the cash and gold income, then lock it away in the safe in the room where I slept.

Only once did I give credit to a man whose name was not on the list which Roy had given me. This was Red Cotton. As soon as he entered the store I knew he had been a 'flu victim, because he was still pale and weak. He offered me a silver half-dollar — all the money he had — and asked me for as much brown beans as it would buy.

I pushed the coin back to him, over the top of the counter, and told him to pick out what he would really like. He chose about five dollars worth of good plain food, which he put in a cardboard box. I began talking with him and soon found he was not the type of person we all thought him to be.

Once the artificial wall he had erected about himself was broken down, I found him a most interesting person and quite trustworthy. Each day, while he was recuperating, he would come to the store and talk awhile. I suspected he had very little real schooling, but had educated himself by reading as much of the better literature as possible. Certainly he knew more Shakespeare, Greek literature, and mythology than most college graduates.

When he was able to work again, he discovered a small bar which was still under water. It was bitterly cold weather, but he set up a rocker and did quite well. In a few days he took out a little more than eight ounces of gold, which I bought on behalf of the Hudson's Bay. Red paid his bill, and left Manson before the onset of winter.

Still another 'flu victim was my old partner Bill. He, too, left Manson in a weakened condition, and entered the hospital in Prince George. While there, he came down with appendicitis, so underwent surgery. The combination almost proved fatal, and it took months before he was really well again.

One other young fellow died of an internal haemorrhage before he could be taken out.

When Roy had fully recovered, I decided I would leave Manson for the winter, so cashed in the gold I had obtained when I worked on the bar. I walked over to the Bert MacDonald camp, because I had been informed the cat-train was due to leave almost immediately, as there were at least six inches of snow at Manson. It was leaving at five a.m. next day, and I received permission to travel with it, so I returned to the store and packed. I said "Adios" to Roy and his police dog "Rinty" and was on my way.

It was around zero when we left the following day. The cat-train consisted of a D6 bulldozer, pulling a freight sleigh, and a caboose. The sleigh was for the crew and their packs, and the caboose, which was nothing more than a tent mounted on a sleigh, was occupied by Bert MacDonald, his engineer, and the two foremen. However, the caboose had a small air-tight wood heater, which made it more comfortable.

It was a sixteen-hour trip to the Nation River, where we camped for the night. The bulldozer cleared the snow from several square yards of gravel ground, and a big fire was lit in the centre. We spread out our bedrolls around it, after eating supper and turned in. It was cold! Quite a bit below zero, in fact. We had not had time to make proper beds of spruce boughs, and the gravel bed was hard and cold. I, and several more, slept very little that night. Only those who possessed eiderdown sleeping bags were comfortable, and I made up my mind to purchase one as soon as I arrived in Fort St. James.

The next day was even colder. Several of MacDonald's crew took turns driving the cat, because it was a little too severe for one man to stay on the exposed seat for more than a couple of hours at a time. Most of us walked behind the cat-train to keep warm. It was with relief, we finally pulled up near Forfar's Hotel in Fort St. James and all went in the lobby to thaw out around the big wood heater.

I obtained a room for the night, because it was quite late, but most of MacDonald's crew travelled by truck to Vanderhoof. It was my intention to stay overnight only, but, unknown to me, Skookum Davidson had preceded us to the Fort by about half a day. I, and everyone else in the hotel, knew it when Skook finally got around to going to his bed around four a.m. The big man, with the big voice, just about shook the hotel to its foundations.

It was always an event when Skook blew into town. Money — mostly his — was scattered around like confetti, and he would never leave town until he was flat broke. He would then disappear with his pack train for a month or more. On his return, he would give a repeat performance. Despite his great physical strength and fondness for rum, Skook never sought trouble. His great, booming laugh was his trademark.

At breakfast the following morning, I heard there would be a dance and decided to stay another day at the hotel so I could attend. It was not hard to guess who would be putting it on. What did surprise me, was when Skook asked me to play the accordion, because the man who usually played would be unable to attend before midnight.

Not many were in attendance for the first hour, but when Skook and his party made an appearance, then the dance livened up at once. All of them seemed a little high, and in no time the schoolhouse was jumping. They wanted all the dances at a fast tempo, square dances, one-steps, and two-steps being preferred.

Every once in awhile, Skook would come around and thrust a dollar bill, either down my shirt collar or under the accordion strap. I played everything I knew for the kind of dances they called for and had to repeat some of them several times over, but nobody cared. I thought they would never get tired, but finally Skook called the "home waltz" and that was it. I returned to the hotel room quite a few dollars richer than when I left.

The next day I returned to Chilco and home. The folks informed me that Bill was still in Prince George hospital, so I thought I would go to see him. He was in the big public ward, and I found it hard to believe it was really Bill when I first saw him. He could not have weighed much more than a hundred pounds. The poor guy must have had a terrific battle to stay alive.

He was quite cheerful and obviously glad to see me. He requested all the information I could give him about Manson Creek and talked confidently of soon returning to his job there. I stayed with him during visiting hours and promised I would be back later that evening.

I was worried when I left him, because I felt positive he could not recover. I sought out his doctor and had quite a long talk with him about Bill. The doctor assured me he was going to recover, but it would be a long time before he could do much work. He also advised that Bill not return to underground work, but stay with an open air type of job if possible.

After the operation for appendicitis, the 'flu had left him with bronchitis. Then he had suffered a kidney ailment. No wonder the poor fellow had had such a struggle to stay alive. Except for the appendicitis, the doctor thought the long exposure to cold, wet work ing conditions had contributed to the other ailments suffered by Bill. I stayed a few days in Prince George and visited with him twice daily.

On my return to Chilco, I sought out big John Reynolds, and we decided to go back in the tie-cutting business for the rest of the winter. Bill was back home in time for Christmas, which made all of us feel better. He puttered around at a few odd jobs, but remained indoors most of the time, because the cold air bothered his chest.

John and I cut our quota of one thousand ties each, and by the middle of March, Bill had started to hew a few. He was returning to his usual strength again and had been doing physical exercises from a body-building course he had obtained. He was determined to return to his old job at the mine on Lost Creek.

I, too, was anxious to return to Manson Creek and left Chilco for Fort St. James during the last week of March 1938. It was still winter, but the break-up was due to start any day, and I wanted to be in Manson before it began.

The Rossetti and Hayward Partners

I contacted the air transport people on arriving at the Fort and was informed a new aircraft was due in a couple of days. Evidently this plane was something a little different from the average bush plane. When it arrived, on schedule, a large crowd was on the ice at Huffman's Point. Bigger than the previous bush planes of that period, it became known as the "workhorse of the north." It was the first of the famous "Norseman" type to arrive at Fort St. James.

The next day we boarded it for the trip to Manson and Germansen. There were nine other passengers, all with heavy baggage, and the two pilots. The skipper was Grant MacConachie and his co-pilot Ted Field. It was a perfect flying day, absolutely cloudless, and because the plane was ski-equipped, it took a very short run before it was airborne. It was in radio contact with the base at Fort St. James while airborne, and the co-pilot was informing them of the exact position at all times. This, too, was something new.

On approaching Wolverine Lake where we were to land, the ice was dazzling in the reflected sunshine, and I think this caused Grant MacConachie to err a little in his approach. We hit the ice with a terrific jar, and the plane bounced in the air again. After two or three lesser bounces, it finally settled, and we taxied to the shore. The pilots climbed out to examine the skis and struts, but everything was all right.

Roy Cunningham, the Hudson's Bay manager, was there to pick up the mail and a few small items. His police dog Rinty was hitched to a toboggan, and Roy loaded the mail sacks on this. Two other men got off, but the rest of the passengers were going on to DeGanahl's at Germansen.

It was a three-mile hike from Wolverine Lake to the store at Manson, but the hard-packed toboggan trail was easy walking. Roy invited me to stay at his cabin because there was an extra bunk available.

Time passed pleasantly, as we witnessed the spring break-up. Occasionally, in the evening, we would walk upstream and visit

Einer Petersen and his wife. They were very keen on playing bridge, and usually it was in the early hours of the next morning, before Roy and I arrived back at the store.

Many men had wintered in Manson, so there was no lack of company, and the store was the usual meeting place. The big wood heater seemed to add to the general atmosphere of good fellowship. Everyone was waiting for the last of the ice and snow to disappear.

Most of the miners had made plans as to how they were going to work their particular prospects during the coming summer, and all were confident it was going to be a good year. Everything seemed to indicate there would be an even greater influx of men, because conditions "outside," although improving were still very unstable as far as permanent employment was concerned. I had not given much thought to what I intended to do. I surmised I would find another bar or bench to keep me sniping for the summer.

However, it did not happen that way, because I was offered employment at a new operation which was to commence a few miles downstream from the store. Two partners, who had spent many years in Manson, had received some backing to set up a small hydraulic mine on their property. They asked me if I would join them, because they had no experience in setting up monitors.

It would be hard to imagine that two fellows so unlike in all characteristics would even consider being partners, yet their partnership lasted until death separated them. Their only similarity was that both were short in stature.

The first, Alf Hayward, was a small, wiry Englishman — genuine Cockney. He loved to laugh a lot, moved fast, had a head of well-groomed white hair, under which was a keen brain. He was a Protestant.

His partner, Sam Rossetti, was of the same height and Italian. He was one of the gentlest of men, quiet and slow moving, with honesty etched in his person. He was Roman Catholic. Everyone respected the Rossetti and Hayward partners.

Before moving down to their camp, I purchased one of the new hard hats, which were just being introduced in the mining industry, because I knew my first job was to be drilling and blasting in a rock-cut. It was one of the best investments I ever made.

In camp, I was billeted with Alf Hayward's brother, named Bill. He was a veteran of World War I, and had been badly shell-shocked. Alf had to keep an eye on him most of the time, because

134

his actions were a little erratic, and this could have led to bodily injury. He seldom spoke to anyone, but he was a good worker. However, when we started work in the rock-cut, Alf impressed upon me that I was in full charge and under no circumstances was Bill to do any blasting. Before I lit the fuses I had to make sure Bill was in a safe place, because the explosions affected his nerves.

After a few days, Alf removed Bill from the job altogether, because he was getting more nervous all the time. To replace him, a fellow named McCullough was sent as my helper, and almost immediately he just about killed me.

It happened this way. We were drilling holes in the rock-face, by a method known as "double-jacking." McCullough would strike the end of a steel drill I was holding, swinging a ten-pound sledge hammer to hit the drill. I was in a bent-over position, and after each blow I would partly turn the drill steel and wait for the next blow.

All was going well until my helper struck the side of the rock wall when he was swinging and completely missed the end of the steel. The hammer head struck my hard hat on the bracket where a lamp could be worn on underground work. My head seemed to explode, and that is all I remembered about the accident.

When I came around, McCullough was staring anxiously into my face, because he had propped me against the rock wall. The metal lamp bracket on my hard hat was completely crushed but the hat itself had withstood the impact. I truly believe the hard hat saved my life. As it was, I suffered nothing more than a slight concussion.

Incredible as it may seem, a few days after this incident I was walking along this same narrow rock-cut when a piece of schist broke away from the rock wall. It landed squarely on top of my battered hard hat and broke in half. Again, the hat had saved me from injury. McCullough, who was a few feet to the rear and witnessed the incident, promptly walked to the store in Manson Creek, and purchased a hat for himself.

At last came the day when the rock-cut was completed, and now we prepared for the hydraulicking operation. More men had been hired, Paul Porter, Don Gilliland, a fellow named "Shorty" Henderson, and two French Canadians, Henri Chavinaud, and the other with the unlikely name of Fred Green. Chavinaud was the cook and Fred Green was designated as my helper, once the hydraulics commenced.

Within a few days we had the pipeline and monitors set up, as the penstocks had been built the year before. The sluice boxes were positioned in the rock-cut, so the washed gravel — "tailings" — could be dumped into Manson Creek. We commenced to operate on three eight-hour shifts, with a monitor operator, better known as a "piper," and his helper to a shift.

We soon exposed a large area of bedrock, because the gravel, or paydirt, was only a few feet deep. Alf and Sam decided to clean up the first sluice box to see how much gold had been recovered. It was disappointing! Only a few ounces. Certainly not enough to pay wages, let alone make a profit for the owners.

They decided to abandon that particular section of ground and move further downstream. On commencing operations, it was soon obvious we were not going to expose any bedrock, because the gravel was too deep.

I did not care for the set-up, because everything seemed wrong for good results. There was fine gold in the surface gravel, down to a depth of four feet, but below that level I could not raise a colour, yet we were sluicing at least thirty feet of a face. In addition, the grade on the sluice boxes was too flat, and the fine gold could not settle in the riffles. Finally, there was very little room for tailings, and they kept backing up in the sluice boxes.

We plugged away on three shifts for a week and moved about four thousand yards of gravel in the process. This ground was supposed to have yielded fifty cents a yard when drilled by the Bob Adams drilling crew, but in actual operations it only yielded about one tenth of that amount.

Again it was a losing proposition, and though we tried to persuade Alf and Sam to hydraulic only the top six feet of gravel, they decided to abandon the operation. Back we moved upstream, to test still another section of drilled ground. We were all despondent, because the whole crew wanted to make some money for Sam and Alf, in addition to keeping ourselves employed.

The third set-up did not take long to erect, and it was here I actually found a small nugget when erecting the wings for the first sluice box. This was a good omen, because we had not commenced washing.

Once the water was turned on, the paydirt washed through the sluice at a great rate, because we had unlimited room for the tailings.

In a few days it was necessary to re-locate the monitor, so the water had to be turned off.

The bedrock in front of the wings was a lovely sight. It was liberally sprinkled with gold, and some nuggets were unique. One was almost like a gold coin about the size of a fifty cent piece, yet was much thicker. I gathered a number and took them down to Sam and Alf.

They were very happy and came back to the pit to help clean the bedrock. There was much gold to be seen in the riffles of the first sluice box, so they decided to clean that too. They took the concentrates back to the cabin for further cleaning.

Just how much gold was in the clean-up I don't know, but from my experience of placer work, I knew it was a considerable amount and more than made up for the previous losses. We were all happy, and the next week passed very pleasantly, because the following clean-up was very good.

Then the blow fell! I was off shift when Alf came to the bunkhouse and handed me my time and pay cheque. I stared at him in amazement. "Am I fired?" I asked. He shook his head. "No, but I have to lay you off, because our backers said they would not be responsible for paying any wages after this date," he said.

He continued, "Naturally we had to report the first two set-ups were losing propositions, and they have not yet received the news that things look better now. I'm sorry, fellows, but that's the way it is."

At this point Sam came into the bunkhouse. There were actually tears in his eyes. All he said was, "You are good boys," then he turned and walked out. Poor, soft-hearted Sam!

Years later I visited him on his deathbed after he had suffered a stroke. He was in the Shaughnessy Military Hospital. He was partly paralysed, but could talk. Naturally, we spoke of the placer days in Manson Creek. He wept when I left — we both knew it was the last time we would discuss those bygone days.

Road Crew

The next day we left the Rossetti and Hayward operations and headed for the settlement at Manson Creek. It was still midsummer, and I had not given any thought as to my future plans.

There was a tiny log cabin on the bank of Manson Creek, which was not occupied at the time, so I moved my bedroll in and slept on the bare floor. It was located on the famous Bumblebee placer claim. The cabin was so small, I had to do all my cooking outside over a campfire.

Fred Green joined me one evening and stayed overnight. There was just enough room for two bedrolls on the floor. Having worked with Fred at Rossetti and Hayward's operation, we had much to talk about.

I was curious about his Anglo-Saxon name, because there was no mistaking his French-Canadian accent. I asked, "How come, Fred, you have a name like Fred Green?" Slowly, he answered, "Well, it's as good as any." Then, holding up his right wrist, he asked, "You see this?" I nodded, because it was obvious to see that at some time the wrist had been broken. "I hit a man so hard I did this. I had to get out of Quebec," he finished. I did not pursue the subject further. The next morning he pulled out for Germansen, because he said he would try and find a job at the DeGanahl operation.

I loafed around for some time, visiting among the many snipers in Manson. One day, another of the men with whom I had worked at Rossetti's called on me. He informed me he could get a contract from Ogilvie of the C. M. & S. mine to supply the mine with a thousand cords of dry wood at two dollars and fifty cents a cord.

He proposed that if I would finance the setting up of a camp, we would share any profits on a fifty-fifty basis. We would hire men and pay them two dollars a cord, which gave us a profit on every cord they cut. In addition, we would also cut wood and make wages.

It sounded good, because we both knew there was a terrific amount of fire-killed jack pine on the Rossetti property, which was still standing. We had no difficulty getting permission from Sam and Alf to cut it, because it would be all windfall in a few years if it were not cut.

We set up a tent camp near the timber and hired the woman cook and three men from the Bob Adams operation, which had gone broke. Bob had tried to run a mining operation himself, without the Ontario backing he had previously enjoyed. It ended in disaster and the crew had been left stranded and penniless in Manson Creek. The three men and the woman cook were glad to find employment with us. The woman had a five- or six-year-old daughter with her.

All went well at first. The wood piled up in neat rows, and after two weeks, we measured the cords each man had cut. I wrote out a cheque to each for the full amount.

To get the wood to the mine, a new road was bulldozed down Slate Creek, and a bridge constructed over Manson Creek. The road then passed through the MacDonald property, then on to the timber on the Rossetti property. Two men in partnership, Bill Faith and Hans Madsen, had the trucking contract to haul the cordwood to the mine.

It was at this time the settlement at Manson narrowly escaped being wiped out by fire. Cinders from a steam shovel were supposed to have been responsible. The whole mountain opposite the settlement was ablaze, and the flames came down as far as Slate Creek. The new store, operated by Charlie Bloomfield, was saved by hard work, because many pitched in to help. The ground all around was blackened by the fire. However, the flames did not cross Slate Creek, so the settlement remained intact.

About a month after the start of our cordwood operations, the man who had obtained the contract informed me he wanted to run it himself. Seeing how I had financed the enterprise, this came as a surprise, but I had no intention to argue the matter. I agreed to pull out of it, if and when, he paid me the amount I had financed.

It took him a couple of days to raise the money from various people. His parents, who were living in a cabin near Kildare Gulch, contributed most of the amount. It was just as well it happened that way, because within a short time Ogilvie put in his own crew of woodcutters and cancelled the contract.

There was much activity in Manson, despite the fact the Bob Adams outfit had folded. The Bert MacDonald steam shovel operation, the Dunsmore mine on Lost Creek, and the C. M. & S. steam-powered slack-line on Slate Creek. In addition, the McCorkell hydraulics and the huge DeGanahl enterprise were running at full capacity at Germansen, twenty miles away.

I watched them all, because I was keenly interested in every phase of placer mining. Scores of snipers were busy trying to eke out a living from the gravels.

A new house had been constructed for the Hudson's Bay manager. Roy Cunningham had been transferred, and the new manager was Bill Murray. Bill was married, but did not bring his wife to Manson. He was addicted to playing poker and could always be found in the game, if one was in progress. He lost heavily at times, quite often to the detriment of the store.

As the fall season approached, the poker games got into full swing. Sometimes they ran non-stop from Friday evening until the following Monday. Occasionally I sat in, but more often I played the part of spectator.

My old partner Bill, who was again working at the mine on Lost Creek, would sit in on the weekend sessions. He was a good player and needed to be, because a number of expert players had drifted in to Manson. Several made their living at cards, and quite a good percentage of the various payrolls wound up in the pockets of these sharpies. I don't think there was any actual cheating, because one night I saw two of these experts clash.

Both were sitting with pat hands, dealt by one of the miners. Each tried to outguess the other and, by back-raising had forced all other players to throw their hands into the discards. There was a large amount of money in the pot. When one had no money left, the hands were laid face up on the table. Incredibly, both had spade flushes, but the one with the ace of spades naturally won the pot. The loser said nothing, but just walked out of the door.

The beginning of September 1938 saw quite a pall of smoke over the countryside. The sun just a red ball in a cloudless, but smoke-filled sky. There were many bush fires burning, but none near Manson.

I was still domiciled in the small cabin on the Bumblebee claim. Sometimes I would do a little sluicing to pass away the time and make a few dollars. The nights were cold, but the days quite warm. It was a good life!

Towards the middle of October I decided to leave Manson to see how things were "outside." For three days I camped at Wolverine

Lake to await the arrival of a plane, because I was not sure of the exact time it would arrive.

On the afternoon of the third day, I was joined by Ogilvie's son Gordon, who was going back to the city to write an exam for engineering in mining. He had a friend with him.

About an hour after their arrival at Wolverine Lake, the plane landed. It was a small Waco biplane and could only take two passengers, in addition to baggage and some freight. They knew, via the radio at Slate Creek, just when the plane would arrive. Although I had been waiting three days, Gordon Ogilvie told me it was very important he get out right away, so I gave up my seat.

The pilot assured me he was returning the following day, but that was not true. After waiting another three days, I returned to Manson. I had barely returned to the Hudson's Bay store, when we saw the plane circling Wolverine Lake just before it landed.

At the store I met Bill Faith, and he said he was taking out his truck before the onset of winter, so I asked to ride with the truck. He said I would have to ride on the back with a couple of other fellows, because there would be three in the cab, including himself.

We left early next morning. It was very cold with a light snow falling. The truck deck was not covered, but we spread the bedrolls and covered up with a canvas. It was a slow, bumpy ride, because the Baldy road was very rough. On reaching the summit, we stopped to brew a pail of tea and eat whatever each of us had brought along for lunch. It was late at night by the time we reached Schumacher Flats, where we were to camp overnight in one of DeGanahl's cabins.

I vividly remember that night. My feet and legs were numb with cold, and as I walked from the truck to the cabin, they seemed more like blocks of wood than something which belonged to my body. Bill Faith quickly had a fire going in the air-tight heater, while one of the other fellows lit a fire in the cook stove.

After warming up, Bill brought in the grub box from the truck and opened a can of wieners. He invited us to help ourselves, until we had a meal cooked on the stove. I, along with others, took one. It was frozen hard, but otherwise tasted alright. Within a few minutes I got terrible stomach cramps. None of the others was effected.

I unrolled my bedding on the floor and tried to rest, but it was no use. Long after the others were asleep, I was still feeling the effects of that single wiener. To make matters worse, I had to keep getting up to visit the outside biffy. It was hours before the cramps finally subsided. I managed to get a little rest before it was time to climb aboard the truck again. To this day I have never eaten another wiener.

On arrival at Fort St. James, I stayed with my folks for a short time, because they were renting a house on the Hudson's Bay property. During the winter John Reynolds and I moved back to Chilco, because we had a tie-timber limit which had to be cut out.

Bill, my old partner, had stayed on at the mine at Lost Creek. He was again working underground, despite his doctor's advice to the contrary.

Chilco was a dead community, because almost all the families had moved elsewhere to make a living. Homes and homesteads were completely abandoned.

John and I moved into an empty house in close proximity to our timber limit. For several weeks we hacked ties. Occasionally we were visited in the evening by one of the old-time resident trappers, who had been at Chilco since 1913. He regaled us with many stories of the early days. However, we were glad when our contracts were completed, and we could leave the lifeless community.

Spring of 1939 saw me making plans to return to the placer fields of Manson Creek. Word was circulating in Fort St. James that a Colonel Ryan had a contract to improve the existing highway as far as the Nation River, then build a new road to Manson Creek, which would completely eliminate the arduous road over Baldy Mountain.

I saw the road superintendent in Vanderhoof, and he told me a crew would be sent to Manson Creek and commence to clear the right-of-way from that end. Colonel Ryan's crew would commence the new highway from the Nation River, and the two crews would work towards each other, because the route was already surveyed.

I commenced work with the crew from Manson, where our camp, comprised of several large tents, was set up near Wolverine Lake. About thirty axe-men made up the bulk of the crew. In addition, Bert Munro was foreman-in-charge, Jack Roberts was timekeeper, and George Ellis was cook. This was the same Jack Roberts I had met on one of the early trips to Manson Creek.

A fellow named Eric Armishaw and myself were chosen to go ahead of the axe-men. By measuring from the centre of the surveyed line, we had to blaze the trees to designate the full width which had to be cleared for the highway.

It was an interesting job, because we were entering new territory all the time. In addition, Eric and I would pick a site where the crew behind us would eat their midday lunch. Promptly at twelve noon each day, except Sunday, we would have a huge pail of tea brewed up for the axe-men. It was beautiful weather, with very sparse rainfall, which made the bush work all the more pleasant.

Finally, when the clearing had progressed several miles, we had to move camp, because too much time was consumed walking to and from work. Pack horses were used to move the heaviest equipment to the new campsite. This was set up on the shore of the fourth Manson Lake. It was a lovely spot and, to this day, is still used as a picnic and camping ground by many.

After a few weeks we heard that Colonel Ryan's crew had progressed as far as Gafney Creek. They were making tremendous progress, because they had a couple of bulldozers and a road-grader, in addition to many men.

The foreman had occasion to send a message to the crew at Gafney Creek, so he delegated Jack Roberts and me to make the trip. There was no trail, and we decided to cut across country instead of following the survey line.

We were surprised to suddenly see a small silk tent set up in the bush before us. The occupants were even more surprised when we called out to them, because they were lying on their spruce bough beds, reading magazines. Actually, they were supposed to be prospectors for the C. M. & S. Company and should have been out on the job.

Within an hour after leaving their tent, we arrived at Gafney Creek. It was a good sized creek, but the water was low. Jack and I removed our boots and socks and waded across to the tent-camp set up on the opposite bank. We delivered the sealed message and received a sack of mail to take back to our camp. After a good meal, we set out on the return trip, but we followed the surveyed line, because it was much easier walking.

The mail was sorted on our arrival at camp, and Jack received a letter from the Royal Canadian Air Force, telling him to present himself as soon as possible for service. The war clouds were becoming thicker in Europe, because Hitler had convinced himself and the majority of his countrymen that his war machine was invincible. He was almost right!

A radio message was dispatched to Fort St. James, and the next day a Junkers low-wing plane landed on the lake to take Jack back to the Fort. It was piloted by Russ Baker, who years later became the president of Pacific Western Airlines and one of Canada's best known pilots.

Jack went on to become a pilot in the R.C.A.F. He survived World War II and chose the R.C.A.F. as a career, reaching a very high rank in the service.

It was at this time that my old friend and partner, Bill, decided to leave the mine on Lost Creek. He obtained work with us, and I was certainly glad to see him again. He moved into the tent I shared with two more fellows. Bill did not look well. His appetite was poor and he tired very easily. The axe work was too hard for him, so the foreman gave him the job of water boy for the thirsty axe-men. The outdoor life was good for him and seemed to improve him somewhat, but he never could regain his old zest and stamina.

Most of the crew spent the long summer evenings fishing. We had no boats, but had constructed several rafts of pine poles. A few were elaborate affairs, complete with seats and sweeps for rowing.

It was on such a raft Bill and I rowed to Boulder Lake, the third Manson Lake. Boulder Creek emptied into this lake, and several men were washing gold along the creek banks. It was a well-named creek, because nowhere have I seen so many boulders in such a short distance. They were a compact mass, varying in size from half-ton to several tons in weight.

There was a little fine gravel filling the spaces between them, and this was the paydirt. Many were the methods used to move these boulders to get at the pay. It was very hard manual labour, but the pay gravel was quite rich in many places. The gold was extremely coarse and mostly in small nuggets.

We visited with the big French Canadian who occupied the lowermost cabin on the creek. His name was Joe Michaud. He showed us the gold he had recovered, also the method he used to move the huge boulders. It was a primitive contraption, but it worked well enough — something like an old capstan winch. We visited with him until well after sundown, and Bill and I made the return trip down the fourth Manson Lake in the moonlight.

144

It was early in August when we met with Colonel Ryan's crew, which was working towards us. It was at a point where the highway is quite close to Manson River. A huge round boulder in the river marks the approximate spot we met. The boulder originally was on the right-of-way, and one of the bulldozers pushed it into the river.

In a few days time there was no more work for the axe-men, because the bulldozers and grader were to complete the road-building to our starting point at Manson Creek.

A winter road was to be built from Germansen Landing to Aiken Lake, a distance of some eighty miles. The axe-men were divided into two groups, some being sent to Germansen and the others flown to Aiken Lake. I was in the latter group, but Bill went to Germansen.

Again it was Russ Baker piloting the low-wing Junkers plane, who flew us to Aiken Lake. Four men and baggage was the limit for each trip. One man sat with the pilot, because the passenger compartment was separated from the pilot's seats by a firewall. The plane was dual controlled up front, and entry had to be made to the pilot's compartment by way of trapdoors overhead.

Russ would usually ask his passengers if anyone of them had flown before. If they said they had, then he would tell that person he could sit up front with him. There was a catch to it, as I found out, when I acknowledged I had made several trips by air.

"All right," said Russ, "then you can do the honours!" With that, he handed me the starting crank. Russ climbed over the top and let himself through the trapdoor into the pilot's seat. I inserted the crank where I had been told and started to wind on the inertia starter. Slowly at first, then gradually faster and faster, until I thought my head was going to burst. The propeller began to turn in jerky arcs, then the motor suddenly came alive with what was to me a lovely sound.

I was pooped out. Winding on that glorified cream separator was hard labour. The plane was taxiing on the lake when I climbed through the trapdoor and collapsed in the co-pilot's seat, still clutching the crank in my hand. Russ grinned, then gave the motor full power, and we were on our way to Aiken Lake.

The further north we flew, the more mountainous and rugged became the country passing beneath us. The familiar mountains of Manson and Germansen appeared gentle when compared to the harsh peaks of the Ingineka area. Russ pointed the nose of the plane to a pass between two peaks, and soon the plane was letting down to land on Aiken Lake.

On a grassy clearing, a tent-camp had been set up by the first parties to arrive. More arrivals were coming at a few hours intervals and continued the next day until all passengers and freight were landed. We all kept busy fixing up our beds and constructing tables, chairs, etc., with anything we could find.

When everything was completed, we each were handed an axe and mattock, and commenced to clear the right-of-way. It was slow, laborious work, despite the fact it was only twelve feet wide. All the trees had to be cut out by the roots, and all sudden pitches or depressions levelled by hand. In addition, the side-hills had to be hand-graded.

One morning in early September, there was much excitement and talk at the breakfast table. Britain and Hitler's Germany were at war!

How the news reached us, I do not recollect at this time, but we knew almost as soon as it happened. A few of the older men were veterans of World War I, and they seemed more excited than anyone. To the rest of us, especially the younger fellows, it was so remote we did not think too much about it.

The work progressed slowly. Each day we had a little further to walk to work and naturally were still further from camp each evening.

This tent-camp did not compare with the DeGanahl camp, where I had spent such a happy time with the ditch-digging crew. No clowning, sing-songs, or nights of laughter in this one. After work, a few of us would gather in one of the tents for a talk. Sometimes the topic was the "new" war, and the old veterans told us, the younger fellows, that it would not be too long before we were involved. I did not give the war too much thought, but in some vague way I had made up my mind that if I did become involved, then it would be in the Air Force. I liked flying and planes fascinated me.

The work on the road was monotonous and wearying, and I think we were all bored. The weather was gradually becoming worse, and the nights very cold. Shore ice was beginning to form around the edge of Aiken Lake. Several times during our stay, we were awakened at night by the roar of tremendous rockslides somewhere in the mountains around us. The camp was in no danger, but sometimes, in addition to the noise, we could feel the ground vibrate. It made me feel so small and insignificant when compared to the natural forces around us.

I was glad when the day arrived on which we received word to pack up and be ready to leave. All the tools were brought in to camp and bundled. Again, it was Russ Baker at the controls of a Junkers low-wing plane, but this one was different. It had a self-starter and was equipped with seats for the passengers, without any partition between the pilot and passengers.

Two of the passengers with whom I flew out had been airsick on the way in when they flew to Aiken Lake the first time. They elected to lie on the floor for the trip out. The air was not turbulent, but a few bumps were felt among the mountains. They both lay straight out with eyes closed, while the plane flew towards Fort St. James.

One of the men on the floor was our foreman Walter Russell, who lived near Vanderhoof. As we approached Pinchi Lake, I noticed the top of the mountain overlooking the lake had been cleared of trees, in preparation for an open pit mining operation. I pointed this out to Walter, still lying supine on the floor, and he decided to take a look for himself.

Cautiously, he raised himself to his knees to peer out of the window. It was at this critical moment the pilot decided to "waggle his wings" to salute the men on the mountain top immediately beneath us. Poor Walter! He gave a gasp and fell back on the floor as rigid as a poker, his face white. He thought the reason for the plane wobbling was because he had got up to look out of the window.

In a few minutes after leaving Pinchi Lake, we were gliding in for a smooth landing on Stuart Lake. Walter was the first to leave the plane, and he swore no one would ever persuade him to fly anywhere again.

Fort St. James was now my home, because the family had moved from Chilco and was renting one of the Hudson's Bay houses. I had been back only a few days when Bill, my old partner, called on me. He and the rest of the road gang had been brought in from Germansen Landing, because the job was finished for the season. I was shocked at his appearance! His face and body were swollen, and he said he felt ill most of the time. He said he was going to get a medical check when he arrived in Vanderhoof. He asked me what I planned to do during the winter and said if I had nothing specific, I was welcome to join him and our old friend John Reynolds in a tie-cutting contract on his father's property at Chilco.

147

For some time I had been vaguely thinking I might make a trip to Vancouver to try and join the R.C.A.F., because I had no interest in any other branch of the Armed Services. The war in Europe seemed to be in a stalemate. There was little activity by both of the opposing sides. Many correspondents had dubbed it "The Phoney War."

Vancouver and Victoria

It was in November of 1939 that I left Fort St. James for Vancouver, though without any specific plan once I arrived at that city. On the train, I met three acquaintances from Vanderhoof, and it was not long before we had a poker game in session. Because gambling for money was illegal on the train, we used the familiar chips. It was an expensive trip as far as I was concerned. I lost a considerable sum before our destination was reached.

On arrival in the city, I obtained a room at the Alcazar Hotel, and for a week or so, spent a leisurely time looking around Vancouver. I was no stranger to big cities, having spent most of my teen years in two very large ones in Europe. Yet, Vancouver in 1939 was an entirely new experience.

Many thousands of unemployed congregated in the East Hastings, Cordova, Main Street areas, and it was impossible to walk a block or so without being accosted by someone asking for a nickel or a dime. Some were definitely professional panhandlers, but most were genuinely hungry and broke.

We, in the country, certainly knew all about being poor, but we had room to breathe and move around, whereas these poor people were prisoners of a brick and stone environment.

Granville Street, with its numerous movie shows, was the favourite ground for the professional "ladies of the night."

Times were gradually improving for the majority of people in Canada. There were still thousands who were having a hard time keeping themselves supplied with the three basic necessities of life.

After a week or so in Vancouver, I decided I would make a trip to Vancouver Island and boarded the ferry at the foot of Granville Street. I thoroughly enjoyed the trip. Arriving in Victoria, I booked a room at the Dominion Hotel, then took a walk around the main streets to take in the sights.

The first thing to impress me was the cleanliness of the buildings, as opposed to the grimy structures of Vancouver. Second was the absence of panhandlers on the streets. There were undoubtedly many poor people in Victoria, but tney were not obviously so. I liked Victoria, because to me there was a serenity not often found in a city.

Maybe it was because much of the time I was a visitor to Beacon Hill Park and spent hours just lazing around, feeding the ducks and seagulls there. It was not long before I found out a poker game was in progress every day in the basement of the Metropole Hotel. I spent many evenings there and, I'm sorry to say, several Sundays.

It was a small game, because a two dollar "stack" would get you a seat at one of the three tables, and fifty cents was the limit of a bet. To me it was a pastime, but a number of young men seemed to make a living at it. Invariably, as soon as they managed to increase their stack of chips to five dollars, they would cash them in. They would return each day and try and repeat the process, and quite often did. If luck was against them, and they lost their original two dollar stack, then they would simply get up and leave the game for the balance of the day. They did not try to force their luck.

I wondered many times if they were actually living together and pooled their resources, so if one had bad luck it was countered by the winnings of the others. Their expressions did not betray them, because they always acted like total strangers.

Christmas of 1939 found me back in Vancouver. Why I returned, I do not know, because I had no acquaintances there. I was lonely and bored. One of my favourite eating places was the Melrose Cafe, which in those days was located on West Hastings Street.

I decided to eat Christmas dinner there. As usual, I was accosted by several individuals asking for the inevitable dime. I turned down no one, because I knew what hunger pangs felt like. A few blocks from my destination a middle-aged man stopped me. He was dressed a little differently, and his accent seemed to be of German origin. I invited him to have Christmas dinner with me, because I did not want to eat alone. After ordering the usual turkey and trimmings, my guest told me something about himself. He was a Belgian, but spoke German as fluently as his native language.

His stories of life in Belgium during World War I made interesting listening. Evidently he had played the part of a spy, rather than a combatant. I had many meals with my new friend over the Christmas and New Year's holidays, then one day early in January he did not show up at our usual rendezvous, the Melrose Cafe. What was the cause I do not know, and I never saw him again.

I debated with myself whether I should return home or stay on Vancouver Island. I had spent quite a sum of money since I left the North, but was by no means broke. Suddenly, I decided I would try to join the R.C.A.F. I liked flying and thought I could train to be a pilot.

I presented myself at a recruiting office, which I believe was on Howe Street. I got quite a jolt, because I imagined they would be glad to accept any physically fit man in his late twenties. All they seemed interested in was, "Was I a college graduate, or did I hold a University degree?"

Evidently no one could hope to fly a plane, unless he possessed some kind of a diploma. How many young Canadian males received the same treatment will never be known, but it is known that hundreds found devious ways overseas to join the R.A.F. Canada's greatest fighter pilot "ace" of World War II, "Buzz" Beaurling, was one of those who was rejected in Canada and worked his way overseas to join the R.A.F. All this, of course, was corrected after the Battle of Britain, when it was proved the farmer's son was just as skilful as the son of an earl, at the controls of a fighter plane.

Germansen Again

Tired of the city, I decided to return to Fort St. James. Once there, I collected my broadaxe, scoring axe, Swede saw, and bed-roll, then left immediately for Chilco. I had no problem obtaining a five hundred tie contract from George Ogston of Vanderhoof.

I joined my friends, John and Bill, at the latter's home. There was a spare cabin available, which John and I shared. They had started tie cutting earlier, but Bill was too sick to continue. None of us knew it at the time, but my old partner had cut his last tie. He spent most of his time lying on his bunk. One day he called me in and showed me the colour of some urine he had passed. It was bright red! I persuaded him to see the doctor in Vanderhoof, because he had not taken a medical check-up when he returned from the road work at Germansen. On his return from the doctor's office he was exhausted and had to seek his bunk. Several days passed, and there seemed no improvement, despite the liquid diet which the doctor recommended.

John and I decided to walk to Vanderhoof, because we both had a little business with the contractor. I intended to call on the doctor, to see him about Bill. When I introduced myself and stated the reason for my visit, the doctor did not hesitate. He brought in a bottle of whitish liquid, which appeared to be in an almost solid state.

"Look at that!" he exclaimed. I looked, but of course did not understand. He went on to explain, "This is a test on a urine sample from Bill. He is suffering from acute nephritis." Again, he could see I did not comprehend. "Bright's disease," he added. I understood that, and I could see from the doctor's expression that Bill's condition was serious. He told me my partner should be in hospital as early as possible.

On arrival at Bill's home, I called his dad outside and broke the news. The nearest hospital at that time was in Burns Lake, so Bill's father contacted the Anglican minister, who drove Bill there. John and I finished our tie contract and had left Chilco before Bill was discharged from the hospital.

It was several months later before I again saw Bill. He had recovered sufficiently to take up light carpentry work near Terrace and never did return to the North. He married, lived in Prince Rupert, and raised two boys. He died when they were quite young, because nephritis eventually caused his early death. After all our trails together, we had come to the parting. His passing hurt — really hurt. I count myself fortunate to have known a man of his calibre.

Spring of 1940 found me back in Fort St. James, impatient to see the last of the winter's snow. I was planning on returning to Manson Creek.

Early in April some of DeGanahl's men arrived at Forfar's Hotel. The cat-train was being prepared for the trip north, because there was still much snow on the highway out of the Fort. I thought I would say hello to some of my former associates, so walked over to the hotel.

Almost the first man I recognized in the lobby was Bull Beaton. Big, bulky, and loud as ever! He was talking to a group of men, who, as usual were listening without any interruption.

Beyond them, I could see a number of men gathered around a card table. I decided to walk over. Passing Beaton's group, I was surprised when he turned around and greeted me, and was even more so, when he offered me the hand of friendship. After our less than friendly parting, when I had left DeGanahl's employment, the new Beaton was somewhat startling.

Even more was to come! Querying me as to my present situation, I said I was doing nothing at the time, but planned on returning to Manson Creek. Bluntly, he told me to forget Manson and return with them to DeGanahl's operations at Germansen. There it was! I was being offered employment for the coming season. I gladly accepted, because I loved the life and the type of work to be found there.

Looking at Beaton's face, it was obvious he had lost an eye since the last time I had seen him. I wondered, briefly, how it had happened, but it was only after I had returned to Germansen that the story was told to me. According to my informant, Beaton had walked to No. 1 Pit in the early hours of the morning. The graveyard shift was still on duty, because the morning shift was not due to take

153

over until eight a.m. Beaton found the monitors tied down with their jets of water aimed at the base of the working face and the operators in the lunchroom. They explained to him the face was due to cave at any moment, so they had tied down the machines and left the danger area.

Beaton became abusive and ordered them back to the monitors or he would fire them. The operators refused to return, so Beaton walked over to one of the huge machines, untied it, and climbed into the saddle.

He swung the jet high on the gravel face when the whole mass collapsed, and he literally had to run for his life.

He had almost reached safety when the leading edge of the slide overtook him and knocked him down.

His face was driven into the rubble. He lost an eye and received severe lacerations as well as an injury to one of his shoulders.

After greeting some of the men whom I knew quite well, I left the hotel. There was packing to be done for the trip to Germansen, which was due to start the following morning.

Eight o'clock next day the cat-train started on its one hundred and forty mile trip to Germansen. It was a pleasant spring day to us in Fort St. James, but in Europe things had started to happen. The "Phoney War" was over! Part of Hitler's mighty war machine had invaded and occupied Norway in a matter of hours. It was the 9th of April 1940, a day to be remembered in neutral Norway.

The trip over the new road was interesting, but uneventful. The cat-train was comprised of a crawler-tractor pulling a freight-sleigh and a caboose. There were twelve bunks in the latter, so we had to take turns sleeping, because it was a three-day trip.

We would walk three hours, then ride three hours. Only the three Chinese cooks were excused, because they had to prepare meals when we stopped. Progress was slow, and it was easy keeping up with the train. The weather was pleasant during the daytime, but quite cold at night at the higher elevation. Eventually, on the evening of the 12th of April 1940, we arrived at Germansen.

Next morning, after breakfast, I was assigned my new duties as powerhouse operator and electrician. My first job was replacing the floodlights and wiring in No. 1 Pit, because they had been removed at the close of operations the previous fall.

The size of the pit was a little breath-taking. The face was two hundred and twenty feet in height and more than three hundred feet wide. Two giant monitors had been set up, the one on the right-hand side had a nine-inch nozzle, and the other on the left was eight inches.

The barrels were sixteen feet in length, and each was fed by an eighteen-inch waterline. Saddles and stirrups were strapped to the barrels a few feet behind the nozzles. It was here the operators sat when the machines were being operated. Climbing to the saddle, a person immediately sensed the terrific power of the water under pressure passing through the barrel beneath him, yet a slight movement on the deflector bar-control brought immediate response from the mighty machine.

It was a little uncanny that such excessive power could be controlled so easily and quickly by the use of a single lever. Boulders weighing half a ton or more could be driven across the bedrock as if they were toys, so great was the force and weight of water ejected from the nozzles.

I had ample time to study and learn all phases of this type of mining, because I had no regular hours of work. I was solely in charge and had to be available at the powerhouse after the generating plants were switched on. Because there was only a little more than three hours of darkness during midsummer, I had much spare time, but naturally as October approached I was at the powerhouse much longer. It was an enjoyable summer!

Chris Beaton seemed to be a different person, and only a few times did I hear him roar in his old familiar manner. On the few occasions we talked, he never used abusive language, nor did he ever mention the incident which caused the trouble between us the first time.

New pits were being opened up, and because they were a considerable distance from camp, I was given the use of a service truck to carry the supplies of tools, wiring, and floodlights.

I was now the owner of a piano-accordion and played many hours outside the powerhouse during the long summer evenings. Sometimes I played in camp, because once a month a supply of liquor was allowed in and quite a number of the boys had themselves a jamboree. There was no indiscriminate drinking anymore. De-Ganahl had clamped down. Nor were there any married couples living in camp on "Honeymoon Lane," because this, too, had caused trouble.

However, when no real liquor was available, a couple of the men had started to bring in various extracts which could be purchased from the store at Germansen Landing. It was this which caused a funny episode in camp, which could possibly have ended in tragedy.

One of the bedrock cleaners always seemed to have a supply of extract on hand. None of the "top brass" seemed to be aware of it, although everyone else knew it. One evening he drank too much, and the side effect was a little bizarre.

The first we knew of it was when we heard a loud yell outside the long bunkhouse. Those of us inside immediately rushed outside to see what the uproar was all about. A number of onlookers had started to laugh at the man who kept giving forth his Comanche war whoop. It was the bedrock cleaner, and he was putting on a startling act.

He was running at full speed around the bunkhouse, his eyes staring and mouth wide open. Suddenly he would stop and, leaning against the corner of the bunkhouse, he would clutch at his chest. Then off he would go again, as if the very devil were on his tail, giving vent to his terrified yell. He was completely oblivious to all of us. Five or six times he circled the bunkhouse, each time stopping at the same corner to feel at his chest, which was heaving from his exertion. Finally he rested against the bunkhouse wall and started to relax.

We approached him and noticed his eyes were closed, although he was still leaning against the wall. Eventually, as his breathing became more normal, his eyes opened and he spoke. "Never again — never will I ever touch that rotten stuff again." He went on to explain how he had consumed quite a few shots of extract, while reading a magazine and smoking a cigar. Suddenly his heart began to thump and labour, and the rhythm slowed until it had almost come to a stop.

It was this which had prompted him to go into his mad flight around the bunkhouse. While he kept running the heart kept beating, but as soon as he stopped, it began to slow down and everything started to turn dark. He said he was positive it would have quit completely, had he not kept running. Finally, his heart speeded up with the exertion, and he was able to get enough oxygen in the body cells to overcome the poisonous effects of the extract and the cigar.

He learned his lesson and never again in camp did he take alcohol in any form. If any of the other boys had thought about drinking extract, this little incident must have changed their minds. No one ever mentioned it, except to laugh about the weird show put on by the galloping bedrock cleaner.

The work proceeded smoothly, and No. 4 Pit was ready to go into production. It was small, compared to No. 1, but it was unique in the fact that it was a hydraulic lift method of mining. Not only was the gravel being washed from the face by monitors, but the paydirt was being hoisted by water pressure to the sluice boxes some twenty-five feet above. It worked efficiently, unless the monitors at the face brought down too much gravel at one time. When that happened, the intake would clog, resulting in the pit flooding.

The pit was very rich in gold where it paralleled the Germansen River, and often I would walk down in the afternoons to watch the bedrock cleaners at work, because each day new areas were exposed.

Pits No. 2, 3, and 5 were also very good, but soon worked out, because they were benches along the Germansen. No. 1 Pit was uncovering a buried channel, as did the later No. 7, and they were much larger operations. No. 6 Pit was across the Germansen River on the opposite bench. It was the only operation which did not pay. It lasted but three weeks.

It was towards fall when No. 7 Pit went into operation. I think it exceeded everyone's expectations by far. The amount of gold taken in less than one month was hardly credible. What the total number of ounces was, I do not know. The chief engineer and his helper did the refining and smelting. I helped pack the concentrates and larger nuggets, to a pickup truck. There were more than two hundred nuggets which weighed over half an ounce each, and the largest was better than five ounces.

Soon after No. 7 Pit opened I was witness to an amazing sight in No. 1. All one day the giant monitors had been tied up with their jets of water aimed at the bottom of the face to undermine it. It was known the whole face was due to slide. It was continually "working" — that is, small pieces were constantly breaking away due to the pressures building up within the mass, which was imperceptibly moving.

A large crack had appeared in the earth many feet back of the brim of the pit. The monitor operators were on duty, but were in a small lunch shack well out of danger, because it was known many thousands of yards were due to cave at any time. The water pressure was kept in the pipelines. It would not be shut off until after the slide had taken place, in case any line was buried — the extreme pressure would help prevent collapse. Many men lined one side of the pit, and one fellow had a small movie camera.

About two-thirty in the afternoon the face started to move. Slowly the mass moved forward, then as it gained momentum a terrific rush of air came up from the depths of the pit and spilled over the sides. With a mighty moaning noise the wall of clay and gravel raced over the floor of the pit in but a few seconds.

Buried under countless tons of debris were both monitors and many yards of pipeline. Ripped out completely were a two hundred foot stairway and a like amount of pipeline leading into the pit from the penstocks above. Hundreds of boulders, released from their clay prison, had shot ahead of the main mass of rubble and, on reaching the washed bedrock, had bounced around in every direction like so many cavorting marbles. It was a truly unforgettable sight!

To me, it looked almost hopeless to clean up such a mess, but eight days afterwards the pit was ready for operations again. Water power was used, and it was done more cleanly, quickly, and cheaply than any amount of machinery could have done.

A temporary pipeline was hooked to the remaining pipes from the penstocks, then two six-inch monitors were set up. They quickly uncovered the buried monitors and pipelines, and repairs were soon made. Some of the pipes were flattened and had to be replaced, but both the huge machines were comparatively unharmed. The eight-inch monitor needed a new balance box, which, being made of wood, was no problem. The nine-inch needed no repairs other than replacing the sprags which kept it fast to the bedrock.

Within a week after the big machines were back in operation almost all evidence of the tremendous slide had been washed through the sluice boxes, and only the largest chunks of boulder clay had needed blasting to break them into smaller pieces. Water, controlled and under pressure, is one of man's ablest and quickest servants. Nowhere is it so admirably demonstrated as in placer hydraulics.

The DeGanahl operations continued until the end of October. The big clean-up began the first week in November. The sluice boxes were several hundred feet long in the No. 1 Pit, and it was a major operation to take up all the steel-rail riffles, which lined the bottom of the boxes. Only on the last clean-up of the season was this carried out. At other times the first sixty feet from the intake were cleared.

By the middle of the month the clean-up was completed, and the camp buildings, doors, windows, etc., made ready to face the long winter ahead. Only the warehouseman George McFalls would be in camp during the winter. It was none too soon. Already, four inches of snow had fallen, and the temperature was not much above zero. Despite this, we had no trouble travelling to Fort St. James. A number of private cars and taxis had been hired for the hundred and forty mile trip.

Leechtown

On the way out, several of the men had said they were going to Vancouver Island to work at a new placer mine which had just been prepared for operations. This was at a place called Leechtown, some thirty-six miles from the capital city of Victoria.

I decided to join them. The prospect of spending the winter away from the snow sounded very attractive. Staying only long enough in the Fort to change and pack some clothing, I caught a train in Vanderhoof the same night and was on my way.

We were greeted, as usual, by the inevitable rain on our arrival in Vancouver. Three of us booked rooms at the Alcazar Hotel, while several others caught the midnight ferry for Victoria.

The next morning was spent visiting the used car lots, because the two fellows with whom I was travelling had each decided on purchasing a used car. They finally made their choices from a car lot on Georgia Street. The salesman was so pleased at selling two cars at one time, that, in an exuberant moment, he invited the three of us to spend the coming Christmas at his home, should we happen to be in Vancouver at that time.

He probably thought he would never see us again, because he knew we had travelled many miles from home and were on our way to Vancouver Island. He was in for a surprise, if that is what he thought, because we did call on him when Christmas finally came along.

After a few days in Vancouver, Jim, the young man who was going on to Leechtown, decided we had better make a start towards the new job, because he had spent quite a sum of money buying a car, and having it repainted. He drove the car on the ferry, and we were on our way. We knew exactly where to go, because we had received previous instructions.

On arriving at Victoria, Vancouver Island, we travelled quite a few miles north on the Malahat Highway, then turned off to a narrow gravelled road, which quickly put us among some giant fir trees. It seemed almost semi-tropical. Moss hung from the lower limbs of the trees, and large ferns and brackens filled the spaces between the huge trunks. Beyond this belt of trees, we emerged once more into the open country, where large areas were logged off.

Getting near to our destination, we again entered a heavily timbered area, and it continued until camp was reached. As the trees closed around us, it seemed a rather gloomy, depressing place. Everything appeared moist and steamy. Certainly the last place one would expect to find a placer mine, yet here it was.

Almost all the employees were former Germansen men, so we immediately felt at home. The mine manager Tony Pini was also an ex-monitor operator from DeGanahl's mine at Germansen. The accommodations were not as good as those we had been accustomed to, but were adequate, providing the wood heaters in the cabins had fire in them. The firewood was green and wet, so we made sure the fire did not get too low before more wood was added. The rain poured down almost every day.

The operation was on a much smaller scale than at Germansen. One eight-inch monitor operated in the pit, and one five-inch was used to stack the tailings as they came through the sluice boxes. Some of the boulders on bedrock were of tremendous size and had to be drilled and blasted. Others were removed from the pit and piled into heaps, by using a gas-driven donkey engine. For the most part, it was cold, wet, cheerless work, but it was a job with which I was very familiar.

One thing which bothered me was the total destruction of the giant trees over the area to be mined. We had to saw them into lengths, then bore holes into them so we could blow them to pieces with dynamite. The shattered logs were then piled into heaps by using the gas-donkey. When the heaps could not be built any higher, they were set on fire. The dynamited stumps were likewise removed and disposed. What a tremendous, wicked waste of natural resources!

A short time before Christmas, I was sent down to Victoria to meet the early morning ferry from Vancouver. A consulting engineer was due to visit the Leechtown operation. It was a surprise to find this person was none other than Mr. Horace MacNaughton Fraser, the man who had hired me for the Germansen placer mine, back in the fall of 1936. On our drive back to Leechtown, we discussed the Germansen operations, because he was interested in their development since he had left there to open up his own consulting practice in Vancouver.

What Mr. Fraser thought of the Leechtown placer mine is not known to me, but all of us working there knew it was bound to fail. There simply was not enough gold in the gravel bench to make it pay. An additional disadvantage was the smooth, argillaceous bedrock without natural crevices to trap gold. The mining layout was good, as were the flumes, machinery, and hydroelectric equipment, but without the all-important return of gold for the yardage of gravel processed, the rest counted for little. I saw the first clean-up and estimated not more than thirty-five ounces was recovered.

Several of us spent the Christmas and New Year holidays in Vancouver. Not long after our return to Leechtown in 1941, Jim suffered an attack of appendicitis. He was in critical condition in a Victoria hospital for a lengthy period, because the appendix ruptured before he could undergo the required surgery.

The mine was still operating, but no money was forthcoming to meet the payroll. I determined that as soon as Jim was able to travel we would return home. He was discharged from hospital near the end of February. I immediately quit the Leechtown operations and drove his car to Victoria, where we booked a room at a cheap hotel on Yates Street. We stayed there a couple of weeks. Jim was in no condition on his discharge to make the long trip by car to his home in Vanderhoof. In the meantime I obtained the back pay due to us from the mining company.

The End of an Era

We left for Vancouver as soon as Jim started to drive his car again, taking the midnight ferry from Victoria. After a couple of days in Vancouver, we left for our homes in the interior. We could not have picked a worse time to travel. It was a nightmare journey right from the beginning, because it was raining heavily when we left Vancouver. We hit rain, sleet, ice, fog, and drifting snow in that order, as we slowly progressed north. The car had no heater or defrosters, and we had to keep the inside of the windshield free of frost by using coal oil, which we had bought at Soda Creek.

Two days after leaving Vancouver we finally arrived in Vanderhoof. The front bumper was barely hanging in position, because we had skidded into a rock wall in the Fraser Canyon, and on the Quesnel and Cottonwood Canyon hills we had used our long-john underwear on the rear wheels to give us traction in the deep snow. We both were very glad to get back in familiar country, despite the sub-zero weather.

It was much too early to travel back to Germansen, so I obtained a job at the Pinchi Lake mercury mine which was operating around the clock. What a fortune my old partner Bill Timms and I had missed by not staking this property when we visited it during our Manson Creek days. However, there is no way we could have known just how much cinnabar lay beneath our feet at the time. It took one of the largest mining companies, subsidized by the government, to bring it into production. Had World War II not happened at all, the ore-body would still, in all probability, be untouched, but the armed forces had required all the mercury which could be produced.

It was a primitive operation compared to later methods, and it is doubtful if fifty per cent recovery was obtained. Native mercury was to be seen everywhere in and around the mill and roasters, especially in the gutters and galvanized roofing. It is amazing so few suffered mercury poisoning under such conditions. Actually, not many people knew anything about the best and safest methods of extracting mercury. The large mercury mines in Spain had used convicts as labourers.

As soon as possible, I returned with the DeGanahl crew to Germansen. It was a much smaller crew than usual, because the government had passed a regulation that if an employee quit the job, then he could not be replaced. They were wanting base metals — not gold — for the war effort. They would not allow any money to be transferred from DeGanahl's head office in New York either, so all wages and expenses had to be met from the value of the gold obtained.

Then one day it happened! Word came from New York to close down and sell everything!

What a jolt that gave us, because No. 1 Pit was still operating and No. 7 had exceeded everyone's expectations. It was very rich — incredibly so! I helped with the first clean-up, because I was off shift at the time. My duties required that I be at the powerhouse during the hours of darkness only, unless additional floodlamps or wiring had to be installed in the pits. It was now midsummer and I had much spare time, so I helped with the clean-up.

When orders came to close down, the bedrock exposed was washed as clean as possible by the monitors, before the water was shut off for the last time. I, personally, felt very downcast by this turn of events. It was evident we had come to the end of an exciting era. It is extremely doubtful whether the Manson Creek-Germansen gold fields will ever again see so much activity in so short a time.

There was much equipment to be sold, so I, with a truck driver, the warehouseman, the bookkeeper, and of course, Mr. Eassie, the engineer in charge of operations, were at the mine for several weeks after the balance of the crew had left. Some stayed around for a time, cleaning the exposed bedrock in the pits, because much gold was to be found in the cracks and crevices.

Chris "Bull" Beaton was one who stayed to clean bedrock, and he made several thousand dollars in a very short time. My duties consisted of collecting all the electrical lighting equipment, including miles of wiring used in the various pits. When off shift I, too, did some bedrock cleaning and collected about twelve ounces of gold in the evenings.

Every day people were arriving to buy up the equipment which was brought in to the main camp. It was sold very cheaply. In fact, some was given away to get it off the property.

Finally, my turn came to receive my last pay cheque from Germansen Ventures Ltd. Mr. Eassie called me into his office and invited me to sit down, after handing me my cheque. He brought out a bottle of Scotch whiskey and poured me a drink. It was obvious he had had a few nips before I arrived. He would never have done anything like this when the mine was operating. Now I was no longer an employee, so he told me some of his placer mining experiences in other parts of the world, notably in South America.

Finally, I got up to leave and we shook hands. The loaded truck was about to leave for Fort St. James, and I wanted to obtain a ride. The road to the Fort was now quite good. No more had we to travel the steep mountain grades over Baldy. The road built by Colonel Ryan was a big improvement, and it joined with the original road about four miles north of the Nation River.

Arriving back in Fort St. James was like entering another world. The war in Europe was now very hot, and the newscasts carried nothing else.

Again I tried to join the R.C.A.F., and again I was turned down. Finally, I made it. After serving in the Army for several months, I transferred from the Army to aircrew in the R.C.A.F. At last I was flying and was sent overseas, but that is another story.

Present road and
Old Baldy Trail to Manson Creek

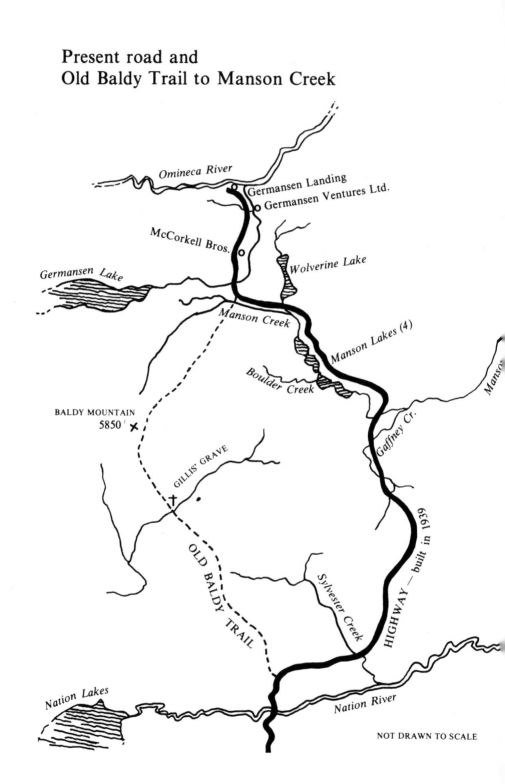

Omineca River

Germansen Landing
Germansen Ventures Ltd.

McCorkell Bros.

Wolverine Lake

Germansen Lake

Manson Creek

Manson Lakes (4)

Boulder Creek

BALDY MOUNTAIN
5850'

GILLIS' GRAVE

Gaffney Cr.

Manson

OLD BALDY TRAIL

Sylvester Creek

HIGHWAY — built in 1939

Nation Lakes

Nation River

NOT DRAWN TO SCALE

Placer Operations

The largest, by far, was the Germansen Ventures Ltd., owned by Ventures Exploration (East Africa), a New York based company with mining interests in various continents of the world.

To obtain sufficient water for the seven pits this company opened, required a twelve-mile ditch and flume construction project. It was a tremendous undertaking, because much of the flume was built on sheer walls skirting Germansen Creek which flowed from the large Germansen Lake. When in full operation, the mine was using one hundred and fifty cubic feet of water per second from the lake, with lesser amounts from Plug Hat Creek and Ah Lock Creek.

Four of the seven operations were on benches along the Germansen River and were numbered 2, 3, 5, and 6. No. 4 was a hydraulic lift type of mining and was slightly below the level of the river. Numbers 1 and 7 were still in production when they closed down the mine. Both were in old river channels which had been buried during the ice age.

By chance, a part of a mammoth tusk was found in No. 1 Pit and, no doubt, other parts had been washed away by the monitors. At least one hundred and fifty men were employed during the construction period. This number was reduced when construction ceased and operations began.

The first engineer-in-charge was Mr. Horace McNaughton Fraser. Later Mr. William Eassie was in charge. Mr. Chris Beaton was superintendent throughout.

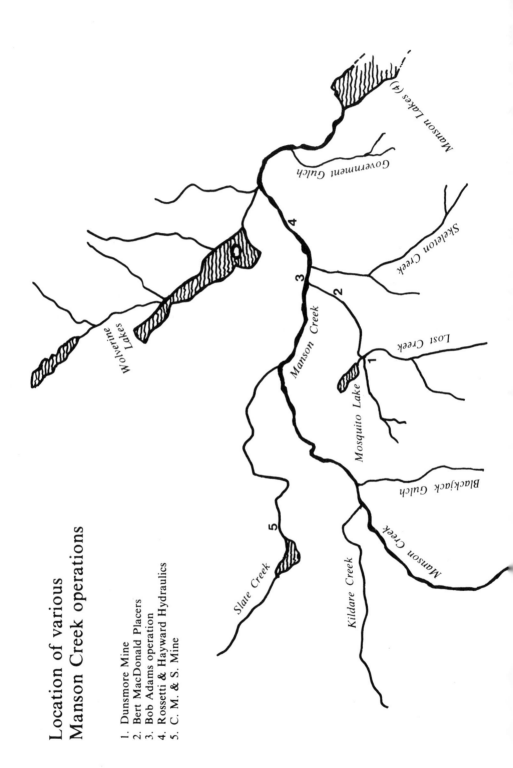

Location of various
Manson Creek operations

1. Dunsmore Mine
2. Bert MacDonald Placers
3. Bob Adams operation
4. Rossetti & Hayward Hydraulics
5. C. M. & S. Mine

Captain Bob Adams

Adams and his drilling crew arrived in Manson Creek from Takla. Using a "Keystone" drill, they had tested a number of areas with little success, until arriving in Manson Creek. He was said to have been financed by the Hammill interests of Ontario. He drilled many placer leases held by local miners, in addition to the ground held by the Rossetti-Hayward company.

When the drilling project ceased, he began his own operation in the creek, downstream from the mouth of Elmore Gulch. First, a huge dam of sandbags was used to divert Manson Creek from the area to be mined. Then a steam shovel was used to construct a bedrock drain to the area.

After excavating a large hole in the river gravels, a hoisting tower was built in the hole, then a grizzly and sluice boxes were attached to the tower. A steam donkey hoisted mine cars to the washing platform on the tower. It was so arranged that, as the car full of paydirt was hoisted, an empty car was lowered to be filled again by the steam shovel working on a twenty-two foot gravel face in the creek bottom.

As the gravel face was mined away from the tower, rails were laid on bedrock, and mine cars were trammed back and forth between the tower and the steam shovel working on the face. Large pumps were used to complete the washing of the paydirt. Although a slower and more costly method of mining, it was quite successful for some time and the gold being recovered made a paying operation.

Towards Fall, a heavy continuous rain struck the Manson area, and the creek reached flood stage. The sandbagged dam burst, and tons of river gravel and tailings quickly filled the excavation. The washing and hoisting tower and plant collapsed and were buried. The steam shovel and donkey engine had been removed before the dam burst, because it had been anticipated.

Adams then moved upstream to a bench on the McCorkell Brothers property, which was still held by them. A similar, but smaller plant was constructed on the bench, the water being pumped from a nearby ditchline.

It was a losing proposition — only a few ounces of gold being recovered. Adams left the country, leaving his crew behind without pay. He never returned.

McCorkell Brothers

This was a hydraulic operation on the benches of the Germansen River, which for a number of years was very successful.

It was owned by Bob and Bert McCorkell, who originally had been packers into the area. Their first operation was in Manson Creek, when they opened up a small channel which was quite rich.

From there they moved to Germansen, where again they found success. The largest nugget recorded up to that time in the Omineca goldfields was found in one of their pits. This nugget weighed twenty-four ounces. Mr. Bert McCorkell, who was in charge of their operations, is said to have used this and other large nuggets as paper weights on his desk.

Their operations ceased soon after the outbreak of World War II, and were never resumed.

The Dunsmore Mine

This mine was on Lost Creek, in close proximity to the Mosquito Lakes. It was unique in that it was the only deep-lead placer mine in the whole area.

The lower half of the creek had been extensively worked by miners of the 1870-71 era. The upper part was an old river channel, which had been filled in during the ice age. The outline of the channel can be traced for several miles, and it appears to cross the present Manson Creek at Discovery Bar, then continues to join the present Slate Creek, and through the Big Wolverine Valley. Certainly at one time it was a very large waterway.

Several attempts had previously been made to enter the channel, and an adit driven by W. B. (Billy) Steele actually did. He removed thousands of dollars in gold before bad air forced abandonment.

The Dunsmore mine tapped the channel from the surface by sinking a ninety-seven foot shaft directly into the centre of the channel. This was made possible by the use of a steam donkey engine for hoisting the gravel to the surface as the shaft was deepened, and the use of an air compressor to furnish air for the picks and jackhammers as well as for ventilation. In addition, compressed air ran the pumps. The mine was successfully operated for a considerable time, and much coarse gold was recovered.

Eventually, the Dunsmores lost their controlling interest, and Bob Dunsmore died of a kidney ailment at the mine. His son Jim moved to Wolverine Lake, where he was stricken by cancer.

The mine did not operate very long after the Dunsmores were removed. Many employees quit, because the new owners were disliked and wages were not paid on a regular basis. Eventually, everything but the machinery was abandoned.

Layout of Dunsmore Mine

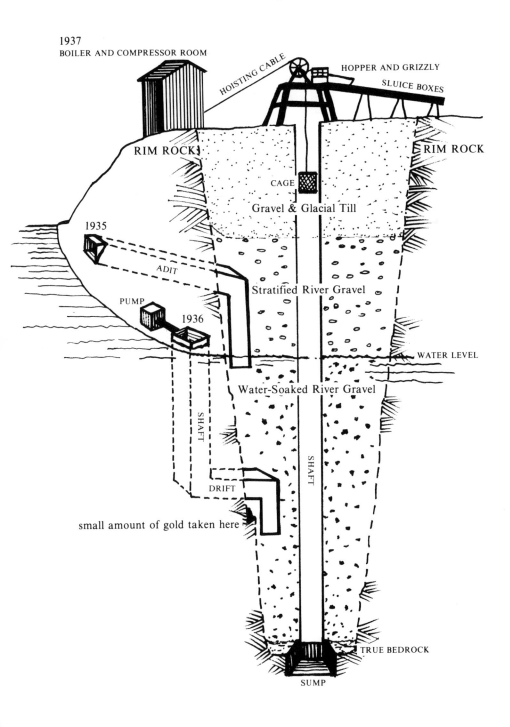

1937
BOILER AND COMPRESSOR ROOM

HOISTING CABLE

HOPPER AND GRIZZLY

SLUICE BOXES

RIM ROCK

RIM ROCK

CAGE

Gravel & Glacial Till

1935

ADIT

Stratified River Gravel

PUMP

1936

WATER LEVEL

Water-Soaked River Gravel

SHAFT

SHAFT

DRIFT

small amount of gold taken here

TRUE BEDROCK

SUMP

The C. M. & S. Mine

— SLATE CREEK

This mine was owned by the Consolidated Mining and Smelting Company, Ltd., of Trail, British Columbia.

The ground was originally held by the old Forty-Second Company who had tried to mine it by using the hydraulic lift method, which was unsuccessful. Later it was staked by Mr. William Ogilvie, who turned it over to the C. M. & S.

This was a tremendous undertaking because all the heavy equipment and machinery had to be transported over the Baldy Mountain Trail. This was made possible by taking apart the machinery, then re-assembling it at the mine site.

The mine provided employment for quite a number of men during the worst of the depression years.

The C. M. & S. thoroughly drilled the ground to be mined. With this advance knowledge, it is hard to understand why they chose the type of operation they did.

Before operations commenced, a number of cabins had to be removed from the area where the Baldy Mountain Trail entered the benches above Slate Creek.

All were removed, with the exception of the one occupied by Mr. William Steele. He refused to move, so consequently he and Mr. Ogilvie were not on friendly terms.

The preliminary work, combined with the actual operations, covered a span of more than six years.

According to the magazine *Western Miner*, the production was $17,000 in bullion the first year and $36,000 the second.

The fine tailings from the mine backed up the waters of Slate Creek and formed a lake.

This was stocked with rainbow trout and for many years provided an excellent spot for fishing.

The mine did not operate after World War II, and much of the equipment, including the upright steam engine, was abandoned.

Mr. W. Ogilvie was the mine manager.

The Rossetti-Hayward Hydraulics

Sam Rossetti and Alfred Hayward held several bench leases on Manson Creek, downstream from the Bert McDonald property. They also owned a placer lease on Government Gulch. After ground sluicing for a number of years, they received backing from an Edmonton-based company to install hydraulic equipment.

In 1937 several new log buildings were constructed. To complement the water supply already being used from Skeleton Creek for their former ground sluicing operations, two small ditch-lines were dug by hand.

A penstock had been constructed, and a pipeline installed before winter halted construction.

Unfortunately, experienced hydraulic men had not been hired to construct the penstock and pipeline, and several costly errors were soon evident when the water was turned on in 1938. After the errors were corrected, three pits were opened, but only one showed real return on the investment.

This pit, which was the last of the three to be opened, was forced to close before the end of the mining season due to lack of water pressure to operate the monitor.

The gold recovered was extremely coarse, and the largest nugget found weighed more than two ounces.

The two partners then returned to their familiar method of ground-sluicing at Government Gulch, where a further thirty-three ounces of gold were recovered before freeze-up.

All camp facilities were excellent, but the water supply to the pits was insufficient to maintain a good hydraulic operation.

The Bert MacDonald Property

This property consisted of a placer lease on Lost Creek and several bench leases on Manson Creek which joined the Rossetti and Hayward property further downstream.

With much financial backing from a Mrs. Susan Littler, Bert MacDonald brought in a large Marion steam shovel. It came to Vanderhoof by Canadian National Railway and took the better part of two years to complete the journey to its final destination at Manson Creek.

The first big obstacle was the Nechako River which was crossed by the additional use of large plank pads when the river was frozen. These pads helped to spread the weight of the huge machines over a larger ice area. By the end of March 1935 it had progressed as far as fourteen miles north of Fort St. James, where a tent camp was set up to await the spring break-up. It was mid-June before the machines got moving again. As it needed a constant supply of dry wood to fire the boiler, a crew of woodcutters had to precede the machine at all times. When crossing the road on Baldy Mountain, it removed many large boulders from the roadbed and straightened some of the worst stretches. These improvements were sufficient to allow trucks to travel under their own power to Manson Creek during the dry summer period of 1936.

On arrival in Manson Creek a washing plant was set up near the mouth of Lost Creek. The shovel dug the gravel which was then deposited on an endless belt which, in turn, fed it into the hopper of the washing plant.

The gold recovered did not make a profitable operation.

Several other bench operations were no more successful, despite the fact that gold was found over a wide area of the benches. It was extremely "spotty" and found from almost the surface down to a depth of three or four feet. The huge machine was not efficient in shallow digging, so fifteen to twenty feet of face had to be worked.

Years later a hydraulic operation was installed further downstream, but this too was unsuccessful.

The steam shovel is now rusted and abandoned.